Cookies!

Cookies!

Irresistible recipes for cookies,
bars, squares and slices

Pippa Cuthbert & Lindsay Cameron Wilson

NEW
HOLLAND

Dedication
To the Charlies, the cookie lovers of the future!

First published in 2007 by
New Holland Publishers (UK) Ltd
London • Cape Town • Sydney • Auckland

Garfield House
86-88 Edgware Road
London W2 2EA
United Kingdom
www.newhollandpublishers.com

80 McKenzie Street
Cape Town 8001
South Africa

Level 1, Unit 4
14 Aquatic Drive
Frenchs Forest, NSW 2086
Australia

218 Lake Road
Northcote
Auckland
New Zealand

10 9 8 7 6 5 4 3 2 1

Text and recipe copyright © 2007 Pippa Cuthbert and
    Lindsay Cameron Wilson
Photographs copyright © 2007 New Holland Publishers (UK) Ltd
Copyright © 2007 New Holland Publishers (UK) Ltd

ISBN 978 1 84537 681 9

Editor: Ruth Hamilton and Anna Bennett
Design: Paul Wright
Photography: Stuart West
Food styling: Pippa Cuthbert
Production: Hazel Kirkman
Editorial Direction: Rosemary Wilkinson

Reproduction by Pica Digital PTE Ltd, Singapore
Printed and bound by C&C Offset, China

Acknowledgements
Many thanks to Julia Leonard at Divertimenti
(www.divertimenti.co.uk) and Lindy Wiffen at Ceramica Blue
(www.ceramicablue.co.uk) for their gorgeous props.
Thanks also to all our family and friends who shared countless
recipes and coveted cookie secrets with us.
Thanks to Stuart West, our tireless photographer, for his
discerning palate and fabulous photography.
And many thanks to Rosie and Eric at Books for Cooks
(www.booksforcooks.com) for their continued support.

Both metric and imperial measures are given for the recipes –
follow either set of measures, but not a mixture of both as they
are not interchangeable.

NOTE
The author and publishers have made every effort to ensure that
all instructions given in this book are safe and accurate, but they
cannot accept liability for any resulting injury or loss or damage to
either property or person, whether direct or consequential and
howsoever arising.

Contents

Introduction

It's a cold and wintry day outside, but I have a cup of tea and chocolate cookies to keep me warm. These cookies, Mary's cookies, aren't your average chocolate cookies. They are made in a saucepan on the hob, with just a handful of simple ingredients. Chocolate is melted with butter, milk and vanilla extract. Oats and coconut are added and everything is stirred together until it forms a smooth mass. The mixture is spooned on to parchment-lined baking sheets, and the cookies are chilled until firm. Strangely enough, the poor things don't even have a name. Some call them "no-bake chocolate cookies". Boring. I've heard them called chocolate macaroons, but really, everyone knows macaroons are baked. I recently heard them called *frogs*, which doesn't make any sense whatsoever, but it's the most interesting name I've heard, so that's what they will be. I try to let my *frogs* firm in the fridge, but I can't wait that long. The cookies are warm and perfect for eating. As I scoop a frog from the baking parchment, I look over my shoulder. A smear of chocolate is left where the cookie should be, and there's no way I can cover my tracks. My mother will know that I helped myself to a cookie before they were ready. But hey, aren't I the mother now, and can't I do whatever I want? I haven't tasted these divine little memories for what seems like forever, and I think I deserve this little indulgence.

I found the recipe for this cookie on a faded page in my mother's recipe collection. When she heard that Pippa and I were about to embark on a cookie book, she promptly brought it over. It's a hard-covered black notebook that is just as much a journal as it is a recipe collection. The corners are curled and the spine has long since disappeared. The recipes inside chronicle decades of family meals, the evolution of her cooking, and the people with whom she shared recipes. I open the book and a frail, faded page falls to the floor. The book isn't that old, but it has had a rough life: it has survived a flood, a house fire, many moves and

countless sticky fingers. The first page, however, is surprisingly clear. It is a recipe for Mary's chocolate cookies, given to her in 1974 by our neighbour Mary McNamara. We moved away from Mary's neighbourhood in 1976, and Mary passed away several years ago. But her memory enters my mother's kitchen every time one of Mary's recipes is being made. Today, her memory is here in my kitchen.

That is the beauty of baking cookies. The aroma wafts through the kitchen, creating a familiar warmth that transports us to another time, another place. This may sound overly quaint and archaic in the fast-food, post-feminist world in which we live. But the immediate satisfaction of cookie making slides into modern life perfectly. A cookie can be conceived, whipped up, baked and eaten within 30 minutes. A frilly apron isn't even required. Before we know it we are comforted, and in turn, we can comfort others.

Cookie comfort comes in many forms. Some people require a daily fix of chocolate. Others simply want a crisp ginger cookie to dunk into a cup of tea. Then there are those who reserve cookie comfort for specific times of the year – shortbread at Christmas, chocolate biscuits on Valentine's Day, lemon wafers at Easter. These are times for slightly fancier cookies and indulgent ingredients. The more important the celebration, the more splendid the cookie, you see. These kinds of cookies not only trigger memories, they reinforce the celebration itself.

English-turned-Canadian writer Margaret Visser writes about the connection between food and custom in her book *The Rituals of Dinner*: "Feasts, by means of structure and ritual, deliberately use the powerful connotations of food to recall origins and earlier times. They also attempt to be events in themselves unforgettable, in order to furnish recollections for the future. The food served at festivals is, therefore, not only richer and more splendid than what we usually eat, but also traditional, inherited from the past and intended to be experienced as ancient custom; the recipes and the lore associated with it are to be handed on by us for use again in ritual celebrations."

I don't think Visser would mind if I replace *cookies* for feasts. Cookies recall origins of earlier times, they attempt to be events in themselves and they furnish recollections for the future. That is quite a lot for a humble little cookie.

The name cookie derives from the Dutch *koekje*, a diminutive of the word *koek*, meaning cake. *Koek* eventually became the English *cookie*. Funnily enough, the name *cookie* is almost exclusively used by North Americans, while the English and French call them *biscuits*. *Biscuit* comes from the French words *bis*, meaning twice, and *cuit*, meaning cooked, which is how biscuits were originally made. This explains the crisp quality of a biscuit. They snap, they crunch and they are delicious dunked in tea. A cookie, on the other hand, is traditionally a free-form drop of dough that is baked just once. The name has evolved to include every kind of "cookie", from drop to rolled, pressed to refrigerated. Bars, squares and slices also come under the category of cookie.

Whichever way you slice it, the tiny cookie carries a great deal of weight. Cookies can represent a country, a celebration, a memory or an event. Their ingredients can be varied according to mood, their flavours shifted according to trends, tastes or availability. They are deceptively easy while simultaneously impressive. That's why Pippa and I love them. They fulfil our varied tastes. They satisfy our cravings. They allow us to celebrate recipes from the past and create memory investments for the future.

Making cookies and biscuits

There are five main methods for making cookies and biscuits. The chosen method basically comes down to the type of cookie or biscuit you are trying to make and is determined by the way in which the butter is incorporated into the mixture. Below we explain the different techniques, and at least one of the methods will apply to each and every recipe that follows.

THE CREAMING METHOD

The creaming method is probably the most common cookie-making method. It involves beating the butter and sugar together until pale, creamy and fluffy in texture. Always use softened butter that has ideally been out of the fridge for at least 30 minutes. The eggs are always added to the creamed mixture before the dry ingredients. Always keep your eggs at room temperature to avoid them curdling with the butter and sugar. If any curdling does occur add a couple of tablespoons of flour to the mixture before adding the remaining egg or liquid. For ease and speed we often refer to using the beaters of an electric mixer for this method but a wooden spoon and a bit of arm power will do the job just as well.

Examples of cookies that use the creaming method are Chocolate chip cookies and Chocolate Afghans.

THE RUBBING METHOD

For this method the butter should be cool and firm but not straight from the fridge. Try removing the butter from the fridge about 5 minutes before you need it and cut it into small cubes. In this method the butter is added to the flour and rubbed using your fingertips until it resembles the texture of fine breadcrumbs. The sugar is then added and combined before the addition of any other liquid ingredients. The mixture will come together to form a firm dough and will hold together in a ball. The dough can then be rolled out and cut into cookie shapes. Sometimes the dough will need to be chilled before it is rolled but the recipe will always specify when this is necessary. If it is a particularly warm day you may wish to do this anyway to ease the process.

This method also works successfully using a food processor. Put the flour and other dry ingredients in the food processor and pulse several times to combine the ingredients. Sprinkle in the cubed butter and pulse several more times (about 10 seconds) until the mixture resembles the texture of fine breadcrumbs. Remove the mixture at this stage and add the liquid ingredients, using a wooden spoon to combine. You do not want to over-mix the mixture by adding the liquid ingredients to the food processor. Mix into a ball and continue as instructed in the recipe.

Examples of cookies that use this method are Sugar butter cookies.

THE MELTING METHOD
This method begins with the butter and sugar (or other sweeteners such as honey or golden syrup) being melted in a saucepan over gentle heat. The dry ingredients are then added to the liquid mixture to form a soft dough. The dough is then shaped and baked, often resulting in a crisp end product.

Examples of cookies using this method are Gingernuts and Flapjacks.

THE WHISKING METHOD
This method begins with the eggs and, more often than not, sugar being whisked together. The dry ingredients are then gently folded into the egg mixture trying to keep it as light and aerated as possible. The result is usually a delicate and crisp, wafer-like biscuit.

Examples of cookies using this method are Tuiles, Fortune cookies and Langues de chat.

THE ALL-IN-ONE METHOD
This straightforward method requires the fat to be soft enough to blend easily. All the ingredients are placed in one bowl or food processor and beaten until just combined. It is important not to over-beat the mixture. Chunky ingredients, such as chocolate chips or nuts, should be stirred in at the end.

Ingredients

BUTTER

Butter is the best fat for cookie making not only for its consistency and texture but also, ultimately, for its flavour. Unsalted and salted butter are both called for in our recipes but unsalted is often the preferred choice for cookie making (when not specified always choose unsalted butter for baking). It is the temperature of butter that is important when making cookies. For the creaming method it should be at room temperature or soft enough to mix easily with the sugar. Remove the butter from the fridge at least 30 minutes before baking for this method. For the rubbed method the butter should be cold and firm but not straight from the fridge. Ideally remove it from the fridge about 5 minutes before you need it. Other fat alternatives to butter are margarine, oil and lard. The most notable difference when using these fats will be the flavour.

SUGAR OR OTHER SWEETENERS

Caster sugar

The smaller crystals or finer grains of caster sugar allow it to incorporate more air than other sugars, which makes it perfect for creating a light fluffy mixture such as you would obtain using the creaming method. The finer grains also dissolve faster, making it ideal in the melting method.

Granulated sugar

Granulated sugar has larger granules and is often used in rubbed cookie mixtures or to make a crunchy sugar topping.

Vanilla sugar

Commercial vanilla sugar is made by adding vanilla extract or vanilla seeds to caster sugar. It is simple and less expensive to make your own: just add a vanilla pod to an airtight jar filled with caster sugar and allow the flavour and aroma to infuse for at least a week.

Brown sugar

When a richer caramel or treacle flavour is desired we have used a variety of brown sugars: soft brown sugar (light or dark), demerara (larger crystals), molasses sugar or muscovado (light or dark) sugars. Brown sugars are white sugar with molasses added.

Icing sugar

Icing sugar is the powdery, brilliant white sugar that dissolves instantly when mixed with liquid. It is ideal for dusting over cookies once cooked or in icings and glazes. Some cookies use icing sugar in the dough, which results in a shorter, more crumbly textured result.

Golden syrup

Golden syrup has a honey-like texture and is a by-product of the sugar-refining process. It adds a distinctive flavour and colour to your baking.

Maple syrup

Look out for maple syrup that has a maple leaf symbol on the label: this guarantees the product's authenticity and its origin. Avoid any "maple-flavoured" products if you can. Maple syrup is the boiled-down sap of maple trees native to Canada and America. It gives a sweetness and yet another distinctive flavour.

Honey

The flavour and aroma of honey depends entirely on the flowers from which the nectar has been obtained. Single-flower honeys are generally the best although some honeys from mixed flowers can also be good – it is all a question of personal taste. The general rule is the darker the honey the stronger the flavour, so choose a honey based on how dominant you want the flavour to be.

FLOUR

There are two main types of wheat grown today: hard and soft, each with a characteristic kernel composition and each with its own particular culinary use. The wheat kernel will vary in "hardness" – the measure of protein content, which in turn determines the flour's gluten content. Hard flour contains large protein chunks and relatively little starch. As a result this flour forms a strong gluten when mixed with water and it is thus commonly used in bread making. Soft flours, on the other hand, contain less protein and a higher starch content and consequently develop a weaker gluten. Soft flours are more commonly used for baking and cakes where the texture is meant to be more tender and crumbly.

The following is a simple guide to the different flours available and their uses:

Plain flour

This is the flour used in almost all of our cookie recipes. Whenever possible choose a grade 00 (the Italian *doppio zero*, double zero) flour, the finest plain flour available, and the one which consequently contains the least gluten. Double zero flour does not require sifting, although sifting is a good habit to get into as it is necessary for all other flours. A harder, or grade 1, flour is also suitable for baking but the gluten level is higher and will produce a

less crumbly end product. Do not use bread flour or strong flour for making cookies.

Self-raising flour

This flour contains raising agents that make cookies and cakes spread and rise, giving them a lighter texture. If you do not have self-raising flour add 1 teaspoon of baking powder to 150g (5½oz) plain flour and combine well. Self-raising flour should not be kept for longer than three months as the raising agents will deteriorate.

Cornmeal (polenta)

A coarse grain produced from the hardest kind of wheat grown today. It is generally too hard for cookie and cake making on its own but can be added to doughs for texture and crunch.

Cornflour

Cornflour is a fine white powder that is often added to cookie mixtures to give a smooth, short and slightly crumbly texture.

Rice flour/potato flour

These are good substitutes for anyone who has a gluten or wheat intolerance and will often result in a shorter, crumblier texture.

RAISING AGENTS

Cookies require raising agents that are fast acting. Compare this to the bread-making process where the raising agent yeast produces CO_2 at a relatively slow rate. In bread making the dough is manipulated enough to allow the gluten to develop. The gluten is in a continuous phase and will continue to expand with the production of CO_2. In cookie making the production of CO_2 is also required to raise the product. The raising is a result of a chemical reaction between acidic and alkaline compounds, and this is where baking powder and bicarbonate of soda come into action.

Bicarbonate of soda

Bicarbonate of soda is an alkaline component and is almost totally made of sodium bicarbonate ($NaHCO_3$, or bicarbonate of soda). It is used when the dough or batter is already acidic enough to react with the baking soda to form CO_2. It requires another acidic ingredient such as buttermilk or yogurt to be present for the reaction to occur. If the dough or batter is not acidic enough then baking powder will be called for.

Baking powder

Baking powder contains bicarbonate of soda and an acid in the form of salt crystals that dissolve in water. Baking powder compensates for the lack of acid in the dough or batter and itself will form a reaction to produce CO_2. A home version of baking powder can be made by mixing ¼ teaspoon bicarbonate of soda with ½ teaspoon cream of tartar; this is roughly equivalent to 1 teaspoon baking powder.

EGGS

For simplicity's sake we have used large eggs, average weight 65–70g (2¼–2½oz), throughout the book. If you find you have an excess of egg whites in your fridge then put them in a bag and freeze them, clearly marking the date and number of whites. Use them within four months. Allow the white to defrost overnight in the fridge or under hot running water and use immediately once defrosted. Frozen eggs should only be used for recipes in which the white is thoroughly cooked.

Separating eggs

Many of our recipes require only an egg yolk or a white. It is easy to separate an egg: tap the middle of the egg sharply against the rim of

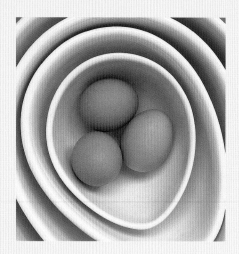

a glass bowl or against the centre of another egg. Holding the egg over the bowl, gently pull the shell apart with the tips of your thumbs. Carefully let the white drain into the bowl while you tip the yolk from one half shell to the other.

CHOCOLATE

Chocolate is obtained from the cocoa bean, which has been roasted, cracked then husked to expose the nibs. The nibs are then ground with water to produce the cocoa liquor or mass. This cocoa mass can then be further reduced to produce cocoa butter and cocoa powder. It is the percentage of cocoa mass or cocoa solids in chocolate that gives it its taste.

Plain and continental plain chocolate

Plain chocolate can generally be made up of up to 95% cocoa solids with no added sugar. This chocolate is extremely bitter, glossy, smooth and almost red in colour. It melts easily and snaps cleanly.

Continental plain chocolate, sometimes labelled bittersweet chocolate, has the addition of sugar and a lower cocoa solids percentage, usually about 50%–70% cocoa solids.

We recommend the use of Lindt chocolate (available worldwide) and also Green & Blacks, an organic chocolate, which is becoming more universally available.

Milk chocolate

Milk chocolate has milk solids and sugar added to it, giving it a lower percentage of cocoa solids – usually about 10%–30%. It is sweeter and creamier in texture, with a less intense chocolate taste. We find that children often prefer this less bitter alternative, particularly in ice cream.

White chocolate

Technically white chocolate is not chocolate at all. White chocolate only contains cocoa butter, milk solids and sugar, no cocoa solids. Vanilla flavouring is often added so look for quality clues on the label, such as "natural" or "pure".

White chocolate is not as readily interchangeable as other chocolate. It must be treated more delicately as it has a tendency to seize.

Chocolate chips/chunks

These tiny morsels of chocolate are perfect for cookie making. They melt easily and are generally more stable than the bar versions of the same chocolate. Be sure to buy chocolate chips made from real chocolate if you can. Alternatively, buy chocolate bars and cut them into chunks.

Cocoa powder

Cocoa is a by-product of chocolate. It is the other product, along with cocoa butter, that is produced when the cocoa solids or cocoa liquor are pressed during the manufacture of chocolate. Cocoa is its dried, powdered

form and has no added sugar. It has a final fat content of between 10%–35%.

FRUIT

Dried fruit is more intense in flavour than fresh fruit. It does not affect the moisture content of the dough so it is usually possible to substitute one dried fruit for another. Apricots, apples, pears and raisins are widely available, although these days it is often possible to find a good selection of tropical fruits and summer berries as well.

Candied and crystallized fruit

Although you can make this yourself, it is a long process and can sometimes work out to be more expensive than buying it ready-made. The process of crystallizing means that the fruits retain their bright colours and can be used for decorative purposes. It is better to buy whole pieces of candied or crystallized fruit and chop them yourself to prevent drying out.

Fresh

Fresh fruit varies considerably in moisture content so it is not as easy to substitute one for another. Fruits such as citrus fruits are often used for their juice and rind rather than their flesh.

NUTS

Nuts can be stirred into cookie doughs before cooking, sprinkled over uncooked doughs or used as decoration on icings or glazes. Always buy whole fresh nuts and chop them as required. They turn rancid relatively quickly so store well in an airtight container and use as quickly as possible.

SEEDS

Seeds are particularly popular in muesli bars and flapjacks, where a wholesome, high-energy product is desired.

SPICES AND HERBS

Spices and herbs are often added to cookies and are an easy way to add flavour. Sweet cookies usually use warm spices such as cinnamon, nutmeg or ginger in their dried, ground forms. Vanilla is probably the spice that is most frequently added to cookies and imparts a fragrant, delicate flavour. Herbs are usually added to savoury cookies or biscuits, although herbs such as rosemary and mint will be found in some sweet cookie recipes.

Vanilla pod

The pod is from a climbing orchid plant native to Central America. Good-quality pods should be deep brown in colour and soft, not hard. Vanilla pods have a warm and perfumed fragrant aroma and taste.

Vanilla extract

When time and money are limited your next best alternative to a vanilla pod is vanilla extract – the "pure" and "natural" distilled extract from the pod. The word "extract" ensures that the product is derived from the vanilla pod. Avoid any imitation or synthetic vanilla "essences". It is the flavour of essences that is used in most cheap ice creams and it leaves a lingering, artificial flavour. Vanilla essence is often made from just one component of vanilla extract – vanillin. It is vanillin in combination with other substances such as gums, resins and oils that make the extract.

If in doubt, always check the bottle for words such as "extract", "pure", and "natural" and avoid any product labelled "essence", "synthetic" or "imitation".

FLAVOURED WATERS

Rosewater is made from the distillation of rose petals and is commonly used in the Middle East and India to flavour both sweet and savoury dishes. This should be available at your local supermarket and can usually be found in the baking section.

Orange flower water (also known as orange blossom water) is made from the distillation of orange blossoms. Like rosewater, this should be available from the baking section of your local supermarket.

Equipment

BOWLS

Invest in a set of bowls in varying sizes: large ones for mixing doughs and smaller ones for measuring individual ingredients. Ensure that they are heatproof so that they can be used over a double boiler or for melting butter and chocolate in the microwave. We like to use glass or Pyrex bowls, which are extremely multi-functional.

MEASURING JUGS/SPOONS

Exact measurements are essential in baking so we encourage investing in an accurate, commercially produced set of each before attempting our recipes. Always level off the top of your spoons using the back of a knife or a palette knife. When measuring brown sugar it should be lightly packed into the spoon and then levelled off. If you are measuring hot liquids use a glass or Pyrex jug that will neither melt nor conduct heat. When measuring liquids always bring yourself down to eye level with the top of the liquid level to check the accuracy of your measure.

Metric measures:
1 tsp = 5 ml (liquid) =
  1 level teaspoon
1 Tbsp = 15ml (liquid) =
  3 level teaspoons

SCALES

It is necessary to own a set of scales with both imperial and metric measures. The most technically advanced and efficient are electronic scales, usually battery-operated, that enable you to switch from metric to imperial at the press of a button. This can be a useful function, but never jump between metric and imperial measurements in one recipe – it won't work – stick strictly to one or the other system. The main advantage of electric scales is that they can be re-set to zero after each ingredient is added. Balance scales require two sets of weights (one for metric and one for imperial). They can be attractive but will take up a lot more space in your kitchen. Scales vary in their maximum weighing capacity so make sure you invest in a set that suit your particular needs.

SIEVES
It is useful to have a large and a small sieve for cookie making. Make sure that they are strong and have a fine mesh. Use the large sieve for sifting dry ingredients such as flour and the small sieve for dusting icing sugar or cocoa powder over cookies.

WHISKS
Wire balloon whisks in a large and small size will be all you need. They are useful for whisking egg whites and whipping cream and can also be useful to help remove lumps from icing sugar. There is also the old-fashioned hand-held rotary whisk, which will help speed things up without having to resort to the electric version.

ELECTRIC MIXERS
We mention these in many of our recipes but don't forget that whisking can often be done using hand-held balloon whisks or hand-held rotary whisks or even a wooden spoon. Electric mixers are useful for whisking egg whites and creaming butter and sugar but remember always to fold the dry ingredients in by hand. Cookie doughs can easily be over-mixed, which will spoil the final texture. Electric whisks are also useful in that they can be used in a saucepan over heat. Choose one with three different speeds and beaters that can be easily removed and washed.

PALETTE KNIVES/SPATULAS (METAL AND RUBBER)
Palette knives are very useful tools that have many uses. They are a simple and easy way to level off teaspoon measures. Also, use them to transfer cut cookie shapes from the worktop or chopping board to the baking sheet and again to a wire cooling rack. Choose a couple of different sizes and knives that are flexible enough to bend under pressure. Rubber spatulas should also

be flexible to enable them to remove every last bit of cookie dough from the mixing bowl. Metal and rubber spatulas are also useful for folding dry ingredients into a creamed or whisked mixture.

BAKING PARCHMENT

Baking parchment is a siliconized baking paper that enables you to bake cookies and cakes without having to grease the tray or tin. Alternatively, you can purchase re-usable baking sheets, which are also siliconized and just need to be wiped clean between each use. If you have no baking parchment the best alternative is to grease your baking sheet lightly with butter or oil or choose a non-stick baking sheet.

WIRE RACKS

Wire racks are essential for cooling cookies and preventing them from going soft or continuing to cook and becoming too crisp! This is because they allow the air to circulate. Once cooked, some cookies should be left for a couple of minutes to firm up before being transferred to the rack. Once completely cool, cookies should immediately be transferred to an airtight container for storage.

ROLLING PINS

Rolling pins come in all shapes and sizes. Some have handles and others don't. Most rolling pins are either wooden or marble, and child-sized rolling pins are available too. Choose whatever is most comfortable for you.

TIMERS

It's important to time your cookies while baking as all recipes are tested and cooking times are given for a reason. One or two minutes too long may result in over-baked or burnt cookies. Most modern ovens are fitted with a timer, but if you are without then it is well worth investing in one. The simple dial timers, which usually time up to 60 minutes, are both cheap and perfectly adequate for cookie making. Modern, digital timers are even more accurate but consequently more expensive as well.

PIPING BAGS

It is worthwhile having a selection of different-sized piping bags with a selection of nozzles. Large piping bags are useful for piping uncooked cookie dough on to trays. Smaller piping bags come in handy when you want to do decorative finishing touches with icing or buttercream. Piping bags these days are generally made of nylon. Choose one that is double-stitched down the seams. Disposable piping bags can also be purchased or, alternatively, use a small plastic bag with the corner snipped off if none of the above are available.

COOKIE CUTTERS

Cookie cutters come in various shapes and sizes and should be sharp enough to give a clean, precise outline. The top side will usually have a smooth rounded edge to press down on so make sure you use it the right way up. Choose metal cutters over plastic, if possible, for a neater finish. It is useful to have a graded set of plain or fluted metal cutters for everyday use but you will find a selection of shapes available for special events or occasions.

COOKIE PRESS

A cookie press looks like an icing syringe and works by forcing the dough through a disc that shapes it into a simple pattern. Cookie presses work best for soft cookie doughs. You will usually find that your press will come with a detailed recipe booklet.

SHORTBREAD MOULDS

The classic shortbread mould is traditionally engraved with a Scottish thistle motif and made of wood. You press the dough into the mould using your fingers and level off the surface with a palette knife. The dough should easily turn out from the mould when turned over on to a baking sheet.

PASTRY BRUSHES

Pastry brushes can be useful for brushing unbaked cookies with a milk or egg glaze or brushing baked cookies with a sugar glaze. The best brushes should have bristles that are securely fixed into the handle. Bristles will be made of natural materials, nylon or even silicon and will come in a range of shapes and sizes.

NOTE ON OVEN TEMPERATURES

Oven temperatures given in the recipes are for conventional ovens. If you have a fan-assisted oven, you will need to reduce the temperature accordingly, by 20°C (68°F). Fan-assisted ovens all perform differently, so always refer to the manufacturer's instructions.

NOTE ON STORAGE

Cookies will keep for 5–7 days in an airtight container or can be frozen for up to 2 months, unless otherwise stated in a recipe.

Chocolate cookies

This chapter is for everyone who believes chocolate is a food group unto itself.

The sweet world is filled with myriad cookie lovers. Some are devoted to shortbread. Others can't see beyond oatmeal raisin. But most, we have to say, are hopelessly devoted to chocolate. This chapter is designed exclusively to satisfy their needs. Here you'll find everything from Chocolate peanut butter pinwheels (page 50) to Lemon and white chocolate biscuits (page 29). All favourites are covered.

But within the chocolate cookie fan base is a group whose chocolate cravings are even more specific. We're talking about – you guessed it – the chocolate chip cookie lover.

The secret to a good chocolate chip cookie lies in the baking. Of course the recipe is important, but an over-cooked cookie is akin to an over-cooked fillet steak. It's edible, but it's just not the same. The science behind the cooking process is advanced, but the bottom line is simple: cookies continue to harden while cooling, so take them out of the oven while they are still slightly underdone. This advice can be applied to most cookies, so take heed. Soft and chewy, that's the key.

Condensed milk chocolate chip cookies

Ultimate

To me, these are the quintessential chocolate chip cookie. I know Lindsay would disagree, but we are from different ends of the world after all!

Makes 24

200g (7oz) **butter, softened**
75g (2¾oz) **caster sugar**
125ml (4fl oz) **sweetened condensed milk**
250g (9oz) **plain flour**
1 tsp **baking powder**
300g (10½oz) **chocolate chips or chunks**

Preheat the oven to 180°C/350°F/ Gas mark 4. Line one or two baking sheets with baking parchment.

Beat the butter and sugar together in a large bowl until pale and creamy. Pour in the condensed milk and beat to combine. In a separate bowl combine the flour and baking powder. Stir into the butter mixture then add the chocolate chips and mix to combine. Roll into tablespoon-sized balls and place on the prepared baking sheets. Press down gently with a fork and bake for 15–18 minutes, or until golden.

White chocolate and orange brownie cookies

Orange heaven

White chocolate and orange is a classic combination. These two flavours set in a brownie-type cookie make for an even better one.

Makes 24

125g (4½oz) **butter,** softened
200g (7oz) **caster sugar**
1 **egg**
Finely grated rind of 1 **small orange**
225g (8oz) **plain flour**
1 tsp **baking powder**
1 **pinch salt**
3 Tbsp **cocoa powder**
200g (7oz) **white chocolate,**
    cut into chunks

Preheat the oven to 180°C/350°F/ Gas mark 4. Line a large baking sheet with baking parchment.

Cream the butter and sugar until pale. Add the egg and orange rind and beat to combine. In a separate bowl combine the flour, baking powder, salt and cocoa powder and add to the creamed mixture. Combine until a stiff mixture forms then stir in the white chocolate until evenly dispersed. Roll the mixture into heaped tablespoon-sized balls and place on the prepared baking sheet, leaving a little space between the balls to allow for spreading.

Bake for 14–16 minutes, or until firm to the touch. Remove from the oven, transfer to a wire rack and allow to cool completely.

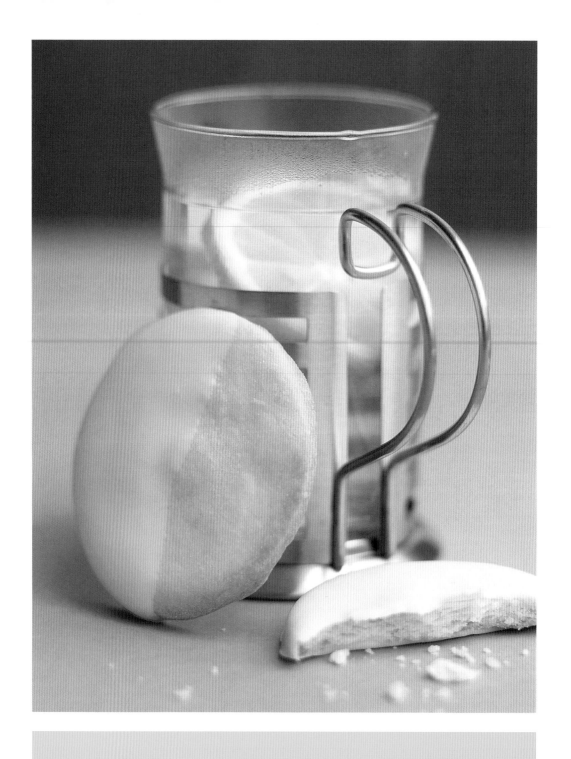

Lemon and white chocolate biscuits

Lemon and white chocolate biscuits

Fragrant

My good friend Emily had cravings for lemon and white chocolate biscuits when she was pregnant with her baby daughter Florence. I have tried to replicate the extortionately priced "organic" variety she used to buy from the local deli. Now you can eat twice as many, Em!

Makes 24–30

125g (4½oz) **butter, softened**
125g (4½oz) **caster sugar**
1 tsp **pure lemon oil**
1 **egg**
450g (1lb) **plain flour**
1 tsp **baking powder**
2 Tbsp **milk**
300g (10½oz) **white chocolate**

Preheat the oven to 170°C/325°F/ Gas mark 3. Line one or two baking sheets with baking parchment.

Beat the butter and sugar in a large bowl until pale and creamy. Add the lemon oil and beat for a further 30 seconds. Beat in the egg until just combined. In a separate bowl combine the flour and baking powder. Mix into the butter mixture, adding enough of the milk to make a dough. Chill if the weather is warm.

Roll out the dough on a lightly floured surface, about 4mm (¼in) thick. Using a 6-cm (2½-in) round cutter, cut the dough into rounds then transfer on to the prepared trays.

Bake for 15–18 minutes, or until lightly golden. Allow to cool slightly then transfer to a wire rack and allow to cool completely. When cool, melt the chocolate in the microwave or over a double boiler. Half dip the biscuits into the chocolate then leave to set on baking parchment in a cool place.

Anita's Afghans

Iced

Anita's Afghans are as much about the icing as the actual cookie. Anita will whip up a batch for almost any occasion and they just seem to get better every time.

Makes 15

200g (7oz) **butter,** softened
150g (5½oz) **caster sugar**
225g (8oz) **plain flour**
50g (1¾oz) **cocoa powder**
75g (2¾oz) **cornflakes**
15 **walnut halves**

For the icing:
300g (10½oz) **icing sugar**
3 Tbsp **cocoa powder**
1 tsp **butter,** softened
3–4 Tbsp **water**

Preheat the oven to 200°C/400°F/ Gas mark 6. Line a baking sheet with baking parchment.

Beat the butter and sugar in a large bowl until light and fluffy. In a separate bowl combine the flour and cocoa powder. Add to the butter mixture with the cornflakes and mix until combined. Shape the mixture into heaped tablespoon-sized balls and place on the baking sheet, leaving a little space between the cookies to allow for spreading. Flatten the balls slightly with your fingers.

Bake for 8 minutes. Turn off the oven and leave the cookies to sit for a further 5 minutes before removing them. Transfer to a wire rack and allow to cool completely.

When cool, prepare the icing. Sift the icing sugar and cocoa powder into a bowl. Add the soft butter and water and mix to form a stiff icing. Spoon a generous tablespoon of icing on to each cookie and top with a walnut half. Leave the icing to set before serving.

Plain chocolate and crystallized ginger cookies

Indulgent

I love a bit of crystallized ginger and plain chocolate as an after-dinner treat, although these cookies are good eaten at any time of day.

Makes 24

150g (5½oz) **continental plain chocolate (70% cocoa solids)**
75g (2¾oz) **butter**, softened
175g (6oz) **light brown sugar**
1 tsp **vanilla extract**
2 **egg yolks**
100g (3½oz) **plain flour**
50g (1¾oz) **cocoa powder**
150g (5½oz) **crystallized ginger,** cut into chunks

Melt the chocolate in a heatproof bowl over a saucepan of simmering water or in the microwave. Set aside and allow to cool slightly.

Preheat the oven to 180°C/350°F/Gas mark 4. Line two baking sheets with baking parchment.

Beat the butter and sugar together in a large bowl until pale and creamy. Add the vanilla extract and egg yolks and beat to combine. In a separate bowl combine the flour and cocoa powder and sift into the butter mixture. Stir to combine then add the melted chocolate and chopped ginger. Mix together. Shape the mixture into tablespoon-sized balls and place on the baking sheets, leaving a little space between them to allow for spreading. Press down with a fork and bake for 15–18 minutes or until softly set. Allow to cool for 5 minutes on the tray then transfer to a wire rack and allow to cool completely.

These are best eaten the day they are made.

Chocolate coconut ganache cookies

Indulgent

These soft ganache-iced cookies are bittersweet and nutty. Put them out for afternoon tea and they wont be around for long!

Makes 20

115g (4¼oz) **butter, softened**
115g (4¼oz) **light brown sugar**
1 **egg**
100g (3½oz) **plain flour**
25g (1oz) **cocoa powder**
1 tsp **baking powder**
100g (3½oz) **sweetened desiccated
   coconut**

For the ganache:
100g (3½oz) **plain chocolate,
   chopped**
60ml (2fl oz) **double cream**
15g (½oz) **butter**

Coconut shavings

Preheat the oven to 180°C/350°F/
Gas mark 4. Line two baking sheets
with baking parchment.

Beat the butter and sugar together until
pale and creamy. Beat in the egg, then
sift in the flour, cocoa powder and
baking powder. Mix to combine then
stir in the coconut. Roll the mixture into
tablespoon-sized balls and place on
the prepared baking sheets, leaving
enough room between them to allow
for spreading. Dip your thumb in flour
and press a deep hole in the centre of
each ball, flattening them out slightly.

Bake for 10–12 minutes or until
cooked. Press the indentation again
with your finger to enhance the hollow.
Allow to cool for 2 minutes on the
baking sheets before transferring to
a wire rack.

When cool, make the ganache. Place
the chopped chocolate in a medium-
sized bowl. Set aside. Heat the cream
and butter in a small saucepan over
medium heat. Bring just to the boil.
Immediately pour the boiling cream
over the chocolate and allow to stand
for 5 minutes. Stir with a whisk until
smooth. Spoon the chocolate ganache
into the hollowed part of the cookie
and top with a couple of shreds of
coconut. Store in a single layer in an
airtight container.

Chocolate coconut ganache cookies

Chocolate salami

Chocolate salami

Rich

This chocolate and biscuit mixture in the shape of a salami makes a great gift. Slice it thinly and serve with coffee.

Makes 1 log

250g (9oz) **plain digestive biscuits**
200g (7oz) **roasted Brazil nuts**
200g (7oz) **continental plain chocolate (70% cocoa solids)**
175g (6oz) **butter**
Grated rind of 1 **orange**
1 Tbsp **Cointreau or brandy**

In a food processor finely grind the biscuits. Add the Brazil nuts and pulse three or four times until chopped but still chunky.

In a small saucepan heat the chocolate and butter until just melted. Remove from the heat and stir in the orange rind and Cointreau or brandy. Stir into the biscuit mixture until well combined. Put in the fridge for about 2 hours, or until cool and beginning to set.

Lay a large piece of baking parchment (about 45cm/18in long) out on a flat surface. Using your hands, tip the mixture on to the paper and manipulate into a sausage shape about 30cm (12in) long and 4–5cm (1½in–2in) in diameter. Roll tightly, securing the ends, and refrigerate overnight or until set. Remove from the fridge 45 minutes to 1 hour before slicing and serving.

This can be kept in the fridge for up to 3 weeks – a great festive season standby.

Chocolate and sour cherry truffle cookies

Sweet-sour

The sharpness of the sour cherries breaks through the sweet cookies – a perfect balance.

Makes 20–24

100g (3½oz) **plain flour**
50g (1¾oz) **cocoa powder**
1 tsp **baking powder**
175g (6oz) **caster sugar**
50g (1¾oz) **butter**, softened and
   cut into cubes
2 **eggs**, beaten
1 tsp **vanilla extract**
100g (3½oz) **dried sour cherries**
100g (3½oz) **icing sugar**

Sift the flour, cocoa powder and baking powder into a large bowl. Add the sugar and stir to combine. Rub in the butter until the mixture resembles fine breadcrumbs. Add the beaten eggs and vanilla and stir in, together with the sour cherries. Cover with clingfilm and chill the mixture for at least 30 minutes.

Preheat the oven to 200°C/400°F/ Gas mark 6 and line a baking sheet with baking parchment.

Roll the mixture into tablespoon-sized balls and drop into the icing sugar. (You won't be able to roll perfectly shaped balls as the mixture is still sticky!) Shake well until coated in a thick layer of icing sugar. Transfer to a baking sheet and bake for 10 minutes or until just set. Transfer to a wire rack and allow to cool completely.

Pecan chocolate chip clusters

Velvety

The chocolate chip cookie in a shortbread, melt-in-your-mouth form.

Makes 30–35

330g (12oz) **butter,** softened
½ tsp **salt**
125g (4½oz) **icing sugar**
1 tsp **rum extract**
1 tsp **cold water**
450g (1lb) **soft flour,** such as pastry
   flour or 00 flour (see page 14)
130g (5oz) **pecan nuts,** chopped
   and toasted
300g (10½oz) **plain chocolate chips
   or plain chocolate,** chopped

Cream the butter and salt in an electric mixer until pale and smooth. Gradually add the icing sugar and cream until light and fluffy, about 5 minutes. Beat in the rum extract and cold water. In a separate bowl combine the flour, pecan nuts and chocolate. Add to the butter mixture and stir until combined. Cover and refrigerate the dough for 30 minutes.

Preheat the oven to 160°C/325°F/ Gas mark 3.

Shape the dough into rounded teaspoon-sized balls and place, 5cm (2in) apart, on ungreased baking sheets. Bake for 20–25 minutes, until the edges are slightly golden. Allow to cool for 5 minutes on the baking sheets, then transfer to wire racks and allow to cool completely.

White chocolate and macadamia cookies
Chunky

This is one of the most ultimate cookie combinations ever.

Makes 20

125g (4½oz) **butter, softened**
225g (8oz) **soft brown sugar**
1 **egg,** lightly beaten
1 tsp **vanilla extract**
225g (8oz) **plain flour**
½ tsp **baking powder**
1 **pinch salt**
200g (7oz) **white chocolate chunks**
  or chips
150g (5½oz) **macadamia nuts,**
  roughly chopped

Preheat the oven to 180°C/350°F/ Gas mark 4. Line a baking sheet with baking parchment.

Beat the butter and sugar together in a large bowl until pale and creamy. Add the egg and vanilla extract and stir to combine. Combine the flour, baking powder and salt together in a separate bowl and stir into the butter mixture until just combined. Fold through the chocolate chunks and macadamia nuts.

Place heaped tablespoonfuls of the mixture on to the prepared baking sheet, leaving a little space between them to allow for spreading.

Bake for 15–20 minutes, or until lightly golden. Allow to cool on the sheets for 5 minutes then transfer to a wire rack and allow to cool completely.

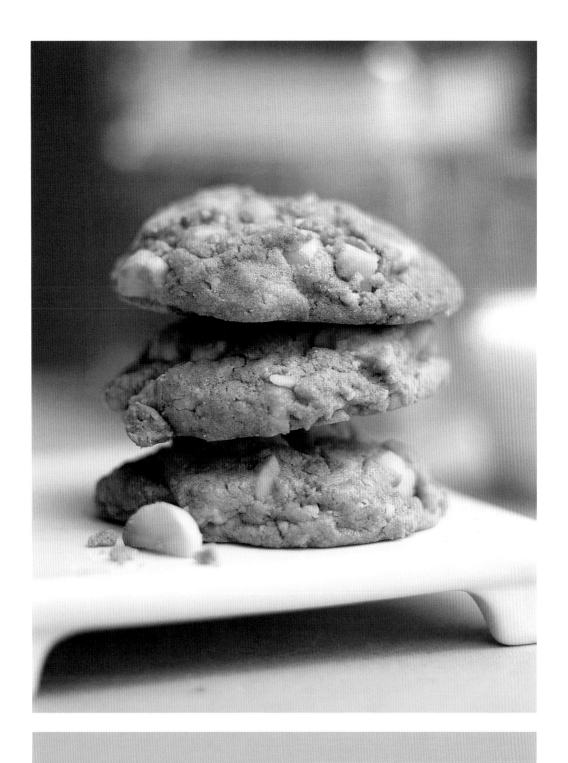

White chocolate and macadamia cookies

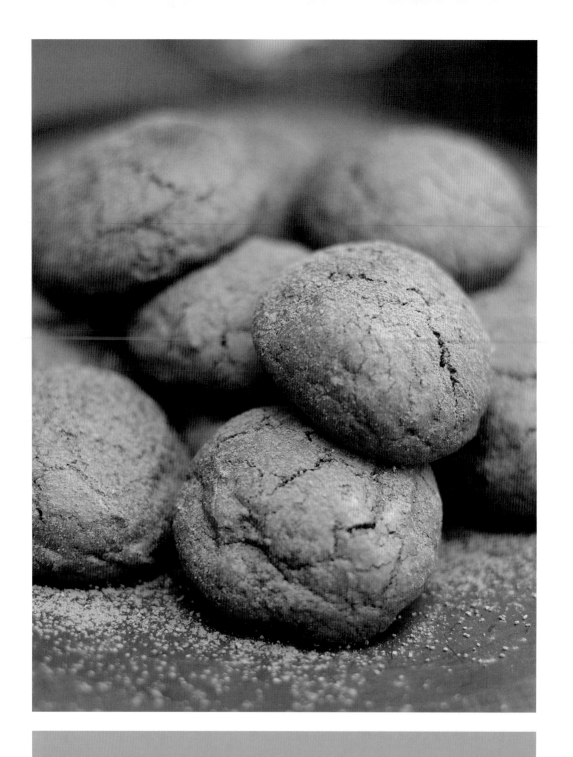

Chocolate truffle cookies

Chocolate truffle cookies

Silky

The slightly crispy exterior of these incredible little cookies engulfs the silky smooth "truffle" within. Use the best continental plain chocolate you can find – the better the chocolate, the better the truffle!

Makes 40–42

250g (9oz) **continental plain chocolate (70% cocoa solids)**, broken
60g (2¼oz) **cocoa powder,** sifted
110g (4oz) **butter**
3 **eggs**
200g (7oz) **caster sugar**
1½ tsp **vanilla extract**
75g (2¾oz) **plain flour**
¼ tsp **baking powder**
¼ tsp **salt**
150g (5½oz) **continental plain chocolate (70% cocoa solids)**, chopped into small chunks

Preheat the oven to 180°C/350°F/ Gas mark 4.

Combine the broken chocolate pieces, the cocoa powder and butter in a metal bowl and place over a pan of simmering water. Stir occasionally until the chocolate and butter have melted.

Remove from the heat, stir to combine and set aside to cool.

Beat the eggs and sugar, using an electric mixer, until light and fluffy. Beat in the vanilla extract and chocolate mixture. Sift together the flour, baking powder and salt. Add to the butter mixture together with the chopped chocolate and stir until just combined.

Cover the dough and chill for at least 3 hours. Even after chilling, the dough will be quite soft. Quickly roll the dough into heaped teaspoon-sized balls (roughly 3cm/1in wide) and place 5cm (2in) apart on ungreased or parchment-lined baking sheets. Bake for 10 minutes, or until the tops are crispy and the centres just set.

Allow to cool for 5 minutes on the baking sheets then transfer to a wire rack and allow to cool completely. Dust with cocoa powder to serve.

The classic chocolate chip cookie

Classic

What you'll find here is a simple round cookie, slightly crisp on the outside, chewy on the inside and studded with plenty of chocolate chips. If you can't find good-quality chocolate chips, use good-quality chocolate, and chop it up into chip-sized chunks. Either way you'll get your chocolate chip cookie fix!

Makes 26–28 large cookies

220g (7¾oz) **butter**
160g (5½oz) **brown sugar**
110g (4oz) **caster sugar**
2 **eggs**
1 tsp **vanilla extract**
300g (10½oz) **plain flour**
1 tsp **bicarbonate of soda**
½ tsp **salt**
250g (9oz) **chocolate chips or plain chocolate,** chopped into chunks

Preheat the oven to 190°C/375°F/Gas mark 5.

Beat the butter and sugars together until smooth. Add the eggs and vanilla and continue beating until combined. Sift the flour, bicarbonate of soda and salt together and stir into the butter mixture until just combined. Add the chocolate chips or chopped chocolate and stir until incorporated.

Drop rounded tablespoonfuls of the dough on to ungreased baking sheets, about 5cm (2in) apart. Bake for 10–12 minutes, until the surface is just set but the centres are still soft. They will appear underdone, but will continue to harden while cooling. The secret is to NOT over-cook them!

Allow to cool on the baking sheets for 2 minutes (no longer or they may harden too much) then transfer to wire racks and allow to cool completely.

Store in an airtight container for up to 5 days, but I've never know them to last that long!

Double chocolate cookies

Rich

These delectable cookies made an appearance in our second book, *Ice Cream!*, where we sandwiched fresh mint ice cream between them. Enjoy them whichever way you like!

Makes 30

200g (7oz) **butter**
250g (9oz) **caster sugar**
125g (4½oz) **light brown sugar**
1 **egg**
1 tsp **vanilla extract**
45g (1½oz) **cocoa powder**
2 Tbsp **milk**
250g (9oz) **plain flour**
¾ tsp **bicarbonate of soda**
150g (5½oz) **plain or white chocolate, chopped**

Preheat the oven to 180°C/350°F/ Gas mark 4. Line two baking sheets with baking parchment.

Cream the butter and sugars together until light and fluffy. Beat in the egg and vanilla extract, then the cocoa powder and milk. Sift the flour and bicarbonate of soda together and stir into the butter mixture until just blended. Stir in the chopped chocolate.

Shape the dough into rounded tablespoon-sized balls and place, 5cm (2in) apart, on the baking sheets. Bake for 12 minutes, allow to cool on the baking sheets for a few minutes, then transfer to a wire rack and allow to cool completely.

Chocolate chip slab cookies

Addictive

These cookies go hand in hand with Wilson family sailing trips, road trips, lazy afternoons at the lake and cosy après-ski winter days. They are a decadent, yet simple, family staple. All thanks go to the Canadian cookbook series *Best of Bridge* for allowing us to include the recipe in this book.

Makes 12–18 large squares

220g (7¾oz) **butter, softened**
200g (7oz) **brown sugar**
1 tsp **vanilla extract**
300g (10½oz) **plain flour**
200g (7oz) **plain or milk chocolate chips or plain or milk chocolate, chopped into chunks**

Preheat the oven to 180°C/350°F/ Gas mark 4. Lightly grease a 38 x 25-in (15 x 10-in) baking tin.

Beat the butter and sugar using an electric mixer until light and fluffy, about 5 minutes (the secret!). Beat in the vanilla extract. Stir in the flour and chocolate chips. Pat the dough into the prepared baking tray. Bake for 25–28 minutes, until the edges are slightly crispy. Allow to cool before slicing into squares.

Chocolate chip slab cookies

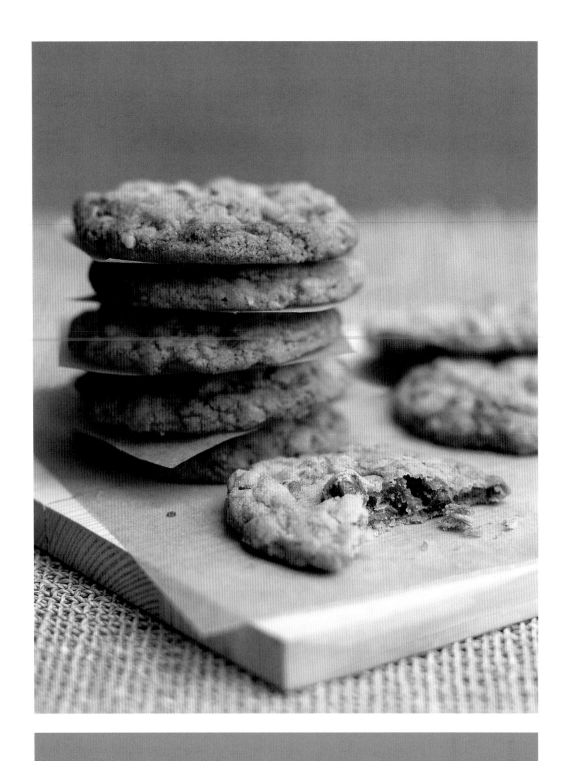

Chocolate chip oatmeal cookies

Chocolate chip oatmeal cookies

Moreish

Crispy on the outside, chewy on the inside, packed with chocolate, slightly sweet and always the first to disappear from the cookie jar. What more can we say?

Makes approx. 24

60ml (2fl oz) **vegetable oil**
75g (2¾oz) **butter,** softened
100g (3½oz) **caster sugar**
110g (4oz) **light brown sugar**
½ tsp **vanilla extract**
1 **egg**
100g (3½oz) **porridge oats**
150g (5½oz) **plain flour**
½ tsp **bicarbonate of soda**
½ tsp **baking powder**
pinch **salt**
150g (5½oz) **plain chocolate chips or plain chocolate,** chopped

Preheat the oven to 180°C/350°F/ Gas mark 4.

Combine the oil, butter and sugars in a large mixing bowl and cream until smooth. Beat in the vanilla and eggs, one at a time, then stir in the oats. In a separate bowl, sift the flour with the bicarbonate of soda, baking powder and salt. Using a wooden spoon, stir the flour mixture into the buttery oat mixture together with the chocolate chips. Stir until just combined.

Drop rounded tablespoonfuls of the dough, 5cm (2in) apart, on to ungreased baking sheets. Bake for 10 minutes, until the surface is set and the centres slightly soft. Allow to cool on the baking sheets for 5 minutes then transfer to wire racks and allow to cool completely. The cookies will firm up slightly while cooling, so don't over-cook.

Chocolate and pepper biscuits

Sharp

A touch of black pepper and a pinch of cayenne add a mysterious edge to these biscuits. Pepper, however, doesn't shift them into savoury territory. They are still a sweet biscuit, perfect with espresso or a cup of tea.

Makes 30

220g (7¾oz) **butter, softened**
100g (3½oz) **icing sugar**
1 tsp **vanilla extract**
220g (7¾oz) **plain flour**
50g (1¾oz) **cocoa powder**
½ tsp **freshly ground black pepper**
⅛ tsp **cayenne**
2–3 Tbsp **demerara sugar, for rolling**

Cream the butter and icing sugar for 3–4 minutes, using an electric mixer, until light and fluffy. Add the vanilla extract and beat until smooth. Sift the flour, cocoa powder, pepper and cayenne together. Add to the butter mixture and stir until smooth. Tip the dough on to a work surface and shape into a 15-cm (6-in) long log. Roll the log in demerara sugar, pressing gently so the sugar will adhere. Cover with clingfilm and chill for 1 hour.

Preheat the oven to 180°C/350°F/ Gas mark 4. Line two baking sheets with baking parchment, or lightly grease.

Slice the log into 5-mm (¼-in) thick slices. Place on the lined or greased baking sheets and bake for 12–15 minutes, until set. Allow to cool on the baking sheets for 5 minutes, then transfer to wire racks and allow to cool completely.

Store in an airtight container for up to 5 days. Alternatively, tightly wrap the dough in clingfilm and freeze for up to 1 month. Defrost in the refrigerator before slicing and baking.

Frogs

Fast

These chewy little delights, made quickly in a saucepan, have many names. Haystacks, frogs, no-bake cookies … regardless of what you decide to call them, they will undoubtedly become a favourite.

Makes approx. 35

400g (14oz) granulated sugar
110g (4oz) butter
60g (2¼oz) cocoa powder, sifted
125ml (4fl oz) milk
½ tsp vanilla extract
⅛ tsp salt
150g (5½oz) porridge oats
100g (3½oz) unsweetened
  desiccated coconut

Line two baking sheets with greaseproof paper or baking parchment.

Combine the sugar, butter and cocoa powder and milk in a saucepan over medium heat. Bring the mixture to the boil, whisking occasionally to remove any lumps. Reduce the heat to medium-low and boil gently for 5 minutes. Remove the saucepan from heat and stir in the vanilla extract and salt. Add the oats and coconut and stir to combine.

Spoon rounded tablespoonfuls of the mixture on to lined trays. Chill for at least 1 hour.

Peel the "frogs" from the paper and store in an airtight container in the fridge for up to 5 days.

Chocolate peanut butter pinwheels

Impressive

I found this recipe in my grandmother's Christmas recipe collection. The pinwheels made an appearance on her Christmas cookie tray throughout the 50s, 60s and 70s. Somehow they fell by the wayside but now, thanks to Christmas-time recipe testing, they are back!

Makes 48

125g (4½oz) **butter**
220g (7¾oz) **caster sugar**
125g (4½oz) **smooth peanut butter**
1 **egg,** lightly beaten
2 Tbsp **milk**
275g (9¾oz) **plain flour**
½ tsp **salt**
½ tsp **bicarbonate of soda**
175g (6oz) **plain chocolate,** broken
1 tsp **butter**

Combine the butter, sugar and peanut butter in a large mixing bowl and beat with an electric whisk until smooth and creamy. Add the egg and milk and beat until smooth. In a separate bowl sift the flour, salt and bicarbonate of soda together. Add to the butter mixture and, using a wooden spoon, stir until just combined. Cover and refrigerate for 1 hour.

Combine the chocolate and 1 tsp butter in a saucepan over low heat and stir until melted. Set aside.

Divide the dough into two equal parts and shape into balls. Flour a work surface and roll one ball into a 24 x 30-cm (9½ x 12-in) rectangle, 5mm (¼in) thick. Spread half of the chocolate mixture over the rectangle. Starting at a narrow end, carefully roll up the dough to the other end. Continue with the other roll. Place both rolls, seam-side down, on a parchment-lined baking sheet and chill for 20 minutes.

Preheat the oven to 200°C/400°F/ Gas mark 6.

Transfer the rolls to a floured surface and slice into 1-cm (½-in) wide cookies. Place on parchment-lined baking sheets and bake for 8–10 minutes, until set and slightly golden. Allow to cool for 5 minutes on the baking sheets then transfer to wire racks and allow to cool completely.

Chocolate peanut butter pinwheels

Bars and oat cookies

Bars, slices, squares. Whatever you call them, they describe the world of flat cookies bordered by a baking tin. Some are simple one-layer cookies, like a brownie or a muesli bar. Others are two layer-cookies, made in two steps. This is where our Pecan and caramel bars (page 71) come in. Some bars reach the three-level height. Bring on the Nanaimo bar (see the recipe for the origins of that one, page 73). All can be sliced according to personal whim. Neatness can be achieved by trimming the sides before cutting the bars into squares or rectangles. Whole rows can be devoured. We like to say we're just making it even.

Sometimes bars, slices or squares can be healthy. That's how oat cookies wiggled their way into this chapter. Oats suggest healthy, right? There are, after all, oat cookies that feature carob and soy. But recipes like these just didn't make the grade. In fact, they triggered quite a debate among our tasters. Should a cookie be healthy in the first place? Some said no. If it's something healthy you want, have a piece of fruit. Others said if you can't tell it's healthy then why not include it?

Our bottom line is simple – if it tastes delicious, it makes the grade. We don't believe in abstinence.

Apricot muesli bars

Tasty

This is adapted from a recipe I developed when I used to work in the Nestlé test kitchens many years ago. As you can imagine, chocolate was in abundance.

Makes 16–20 bars

150g (5½oz) **dried apricots,** chopped into quarters
125ml (4fl oz) **water**
150g (5½oz) **butter,** softened
175g (6oz) **light brown sugar**
150g (5½oz) **plain flour**
1 tsp **baking powder**
100g (3½oz) **porridge oats**
100g (3½oz) **plain, milk or white chocolate,** finely chopped

Preheat the oven to 170°C/325°F/Gas mark 3. Line the base of a 27 x 18 x 3-cm (10¾ x 7 x 1¼-in) shallow baking tin with baking parchment.

Put the apricots and water in a small saucepan. Bring to the boil, reduce the heat and simmer until all the liquid has been absorbed. Remove from the heat and stir in the butter until melted. Add the sugar, stir to combine and allow to cool.

Combine the flour and baking powder and add to the cooled mixture with the oats and chocolate. Press into the tin and bake for 30–35 minutes, or until a skewer inserted comes out clean. Allow to cool in the tin for about 10 minutes then turn out on to a wire rack and allow to cool completely. Cut into bars or squares to serve.

Pecan and ginger oatcakes

Chunky

These are not for the sweet-toothed but they are delicious and make a great snack for kids with a glass of milk on the side.

Makes 15–18

150g (5½oz) **unsalted butter,** softened
75g (2¾oz) **caster sugar**
1 **large egg**
100g (3½oz) **pecan nuts,**
  roughly chopped
2 **pieces stem ginger** (about
  40–50g/1½–1¾oz)
125g (4½oz) **plain flour**
75g (2¾oz) **porridge oats**
1 pinch **salt**
2 Tbsp **demerara sugar**

Preheat the oven to 180°C/350°F/ Gas mark 4. Grease or line a large baking sheet.

Cream the butter and sugar until pale, then beat in the egg. Fold in the nuts, stem ginger, flour, oats and salt. Drop heaped tablespoonfuls of the mixture on to the baking sheet and gently flatten to approximately 1cm (½in) thick. Sprinkle the sugar over the biscuits and bake for 15–18 minutes, or until golden around the edges and lightly golden on top. Transfer to a wire rack and allow to cool completely.

Anakiwa flapjacks

Substantial

This recipe is based on the energy-giving bars I became very addicted to when I did Outward Bound in Anakiwa, New Zealand. This is the British version of a flapjack. In North America, a flapjack refers to a thick pancake cooked on a griddle – so don't be confused.

Makes 8–16

125g (4½oz) **butter**
75ml (2½fl oz) **golden syrup**
1 tsp **bicarbonate of soda**
1 Tbsp **water**
75g (2¾oz) **porridge oats**
75g (2¾oz) **sultanas**
150g (5½oz) **plain flour**
75g (2¾oz) **sunflower seeds,**
    roasted for 8–10 minutes at
    180°C/350°F/Gas mark 4
50g (1¾oz) **sweetened desiccated**
    coconut
100g (3½oz) **demerara sugar**
150g (5½oz) **dried apricots,** chopped

Preheat the oven to 170°C/325°F/Gas mark 3. Line the base and sides of a 27 x 18-cm (10¾ x 7-in) shallow baking tin.

Put the butter and golden syrup in a saucepan over low heat until the butter has melted. Dissolve the bicarbonate of soda in 1 Tbsp boiling water and add to the butter mixture. Stir until the mixture foams then set aside.

In a large bowl combine all the remaining ingredients. Pour over the bicarbonate of soda mixture and stir well until all the dry ingredients are combined. Tip the mixture into the prepared baking tin and press down firmly. Bake for about 30 minutes, or until golden and firm to touch. Allow to cool in the tin before cutting into bars.

Anakiwa flapjacks

White chocolate, cranberry and oat cookies

Balanced

Sweet chocolate, sharp cranberries and savoury oats make for a blissful combination.

Makes 24–30

200g (7oz) **butter, softened**
200g (7oz) **light brown muscovado sugar**
125ml (4fl oz) **sweetened condensed milk**
1 **large egg**
1 tsp **vanilla extract**
200g (7oz) **plain flour**
½ tsp **bicarbonate of soda**
150g (5½oz) **porridge oats**
150g (5½oz) **dried cranberries**
100g (3½oz) **white chocolate chips or buttons**

Preheat the oven to 160°C/325°F/Gas mark 3. Grease two baking sheets or line with baking parchment.

Cream the butter and sugar in a medium bowl until pale and smooth. Add the condensed milk, egg and vanilla extract and beat to combine until light and fluffy.

Combine the flour and bicarbonate of soda together and stir into the creamed mixture. Stir in the oats, cranberries and chocolate chips. Place heaped tablespoonfuls of the mixture on to the prepared baking sheets, leaving a little space between them to allow for spreading, and press them down gently with a fork.

Bake for 15–18 minutes, or until golden brown. Allow to cool for 5 minutes on the baking sheet then transfer to a wire rack and allow to cool completely.

Dream bars

Simplicity

So-called because you can choose your favourite toppings and it will work every time!

___

Makes 16–20

175g (6oz) **plain biscuit crumbs**
75g (2¾oz) **butter,** melted
150g (5½oz) **chocolate chunks
  or chips**
150g (5½oz) **chopped dates**
75g (2¾oz) **dried apricots,** chopped
50g (1¾oz) **sweetened desiccated
  coconut**
50g (1¾oz) **flaked almonds**
1 x 397-g (14-oz) can **sweetened
  condensed milk**

Preheat the oven to 180°C/350°F/ Gas mark 4. Line the base of an 18 x 27-cm (7 x 10 ¾-in) shallow baking tin with baking parchment.

Combine the biscuit crumbs and melted butter and pour into the tin. Press into the tin, using the back of a spoon, until even and smooth. Sprinkle the chocolate, dates, apricots and coconut evenly over the base. Top with the flaked almonds then evenly drizzle over the condensed milk.

Bake in the oven for 25–30 minutes, or until golden on top. Allow to cool in the tin then slice into squares or bars before eating.

Ginger crunch

Ginger crunch

Delectable

This extra thick ginger slice is my nemesis. A perfect accompaniment to a good flat white coffee!

Makes 16–24

For the base:
225g (8oz) **plain flour**
100g (3½oz) **caster sugar**
1 tsp **baking powder**
2 tsp **ground ginger**
150g (5½oz) **butter,** cut into cubes

For the icing:
150g (5½oz) **butter**
60ml (2fl oz) **golden syrup**
300g (10½oz) **icing sugar,** sifted
2 Tbsp **ground ginger**

Preheat the oven to 180°C/350°F/ Gas mark 4. Line a deep-sided 18 x 27-cm (7 x 10¾-in) shallow baking tin with baking parchment.

To make the base, put the flour, sugar, baking powder and ginger in a food processor. Pulse several times to combine then add the butter. Process for about 30 seconds, or until the mixture resembles fine breadcrumbs. This can also be done by hand. Press the mixture evenly into the tin and level off, using the back of a spoon.

Bake for 20–25 minutes, or until lightly golden. Remove from the oven and allow to cool completely.

To make the icing, put the butter and golden syrup in a medium saucepan and heat until just melted. Add the sifted icing sugar and ginger and cook for a further 1–2 minutes, stirring constantly until smooth. Remove from the heat and poor over the base. Leave to set. Remove from the tin and cut into squares or triangles to serve.

Date and hazelnut crumble slice

Textured

This one's for Mum. It makes a good substitute for dessert when served with a generous dollop of crème fraîche or yogurt and is equally good for morning or afternoon tea.

Makes 8–16

For the filling:
400g (14oz) **dried stoned dates,** roughly chopped
Grated rind of 2 **lemons**
250ml (9fl oz) **water**
75g (2¾oz) **sugar**

For the base:
225g (8oz) **plain flour**
100g (3½oz) **caster sugar**
1 tsp **baking powder**
125g (4½oz) **firm butter,** cut into chunks

For the crumble topping:
100g (3½oz) **plain flour**
50g (1¾oz) **light brown sugar**
75g (2¾oz) **hazelnuts,** roughly chopped
75g (2¾oz) **firm butter**

Preheat the oven to 200°C/400°F/ Gas mark 6 and line an 18 x 27-cm (7 x 10 ¾-in) baking tin with baking parchment.

Put the filling ingredients in a saucepan and bring to the boil. Reduce the heat and simmer for 10–15 minutes, or until thick. Allow to cool.

Mix together the flour, caster sugar and baking powder for the base. Using your hands or a food processor, rub in the butter to resemble fine breadcrumbs. Press the mixture firmly into the tin and bake for 15–18 minutes, or until brown around the edges. Remove from the oven.

Combine the crumble ingredients together in another bowl until the mixture is crumbly. Spread the date mixture over the cooked base then sprinkle over the crumble mixture, pressing it down firmly but gently. Return to the oven and cook for a further 15–20 minutes, or until the crumble topping is golden. Allow to cool completely in the tin before serving or serve warm with a spoonful of vanilla ice cream.

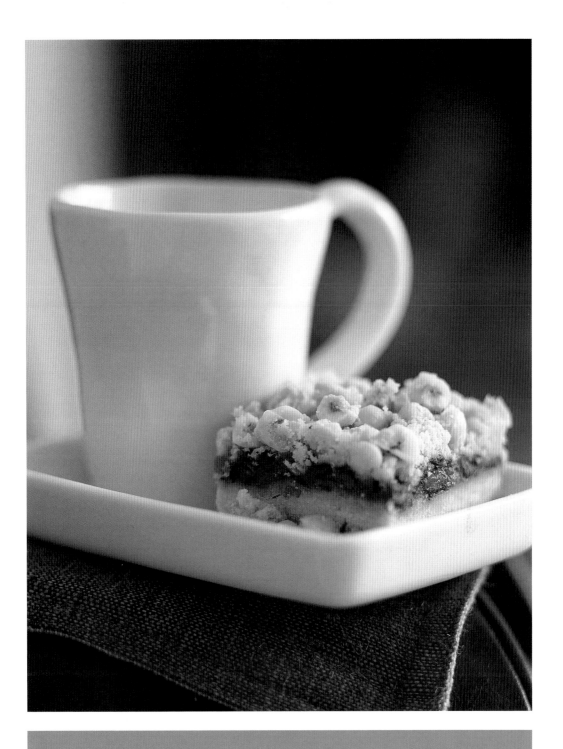

Date and hazelnut crumble slice

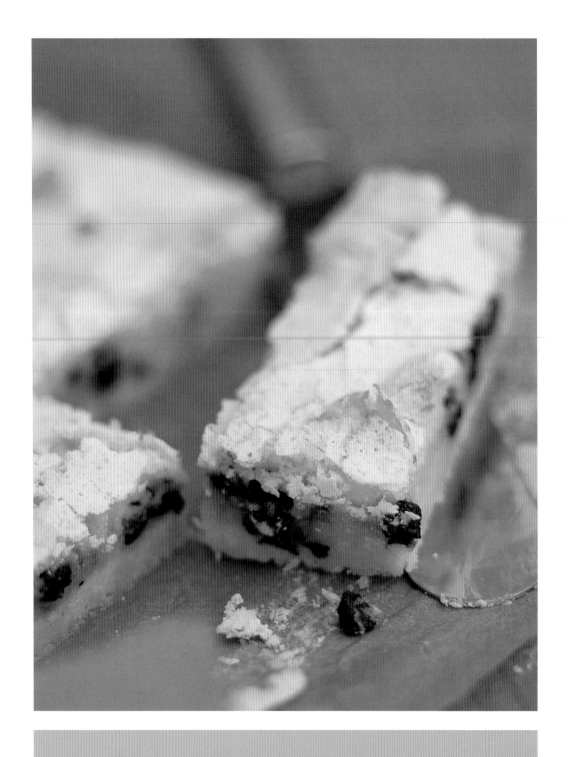

Lemon and blueberry shortcake slice

Lemon and blueberry shortcake slice
Paradise

These have a gooey, lemon curd-like centre with a crispy meringue-like crust. Delicious and our photographer Stuart's favourite!

Makes 16–20

For the base:
225g (8oz) **plain flour**
100g (3½oz) **caster sugar**
175g (6oz) **firm butter,** cut into cubes

For the topping:
3 **eggs**
225g (8oz) **caster sugar, for the base**
Juice (about 100ml/3½fl oz)
    and grated **rind of** 3 **lemons**
40g (1½oz) **flour**
75g (2¾oz) **dried blueberries**
    (optional)
Icing sugar, to serve (optional)

Preheat the oven to 180°C/350°F/ Gas mark 4. Line the base and sides of an 18 x 27-cm (7 x 10¾-in) tin with baking parchment.

Put the flour and the first measure of sugar in a large bowl or food processor and mix to combine. Add the butter and rub together or process until the mixture resembles fine breadcrumbs. Press the crumbs evenly into the prepared tin and bake for 20–25 minutes, or until golden. Remove and reduce the temperature to 140°C/275°F/Gas mark 1.

While the base is cooking, whisk together the eggs and the second measure of sugar, using an electric mixer, until very thick and pale, about 8–10 minutes. Stir in the lemon juice and rind then fold in the flour. Sprinkle the blueberries evenly over the base, if using. Pour over the egg mixture and bake for 35–40 minutes, or until set. Allow to cool in the tin before cutting into bars. Serve dusted with icing sugar, if liked.

■ *Try stirring fresh blueberries into the lemon topping before baking instead of dried.*

Coconut and jam slice

Sticky

This slice is often referred to as Louise cake – but who's Louise? I've kept its name simple so you know exactly what you're getting. It is loved by young and old alike.

Makes approx. 20 triangles

For the base:
175g (6oz) **caster sugar**
115g (4¼oz) **butter,** softened
2 **eggs,** separated
½ tsp **vanilla extract**
225g (8oz) **plain flour**
1 tsp **baking powder**

For the topping:
150g (5½oz) **raspberry jam**
100g (3½oz) **caster sugar**
40g (1½oz) **sweetened desiccated coconut**

Preheat the oven to 160°C/325°F/ Gas mark 3. Line the base of a 18 x 27-cm (7 x 10¾-in), baking tin with baking parchment and set aside.

To make the base, beat the sugar and butter until creamy and pale. Beat in the egg yolks and vanilla extract then add the flour and baking powder. Combine together to form a stiff mixture and press into the prepared tin. Spread the raw base with the raspberry jam. Using clean beaters, beat the egg whites until soft peaks form, then beat in the second measure of sugar and continue beating until the mixture forms a glossy meringue. Fold in the coconut and spread evenly over the jam and base.

Bake for about 1 hour, or until crisp and golden. Cut the slice into triangles while still warm.

Energizing muesli bars

Sweet fuel

These bars straddle the fence between a tasty, energy bar packed with treats and goodness, and a decadent bar worthy of dessert status. Either way, the inspiration for this recipe is thanks to family friend and fine baker Sandra Nowlan.

Makes approx. 25 squares

110g (4oz) **butter,** melted
80g (3oz) **light brown sugar**
80ml (2½fl oz) **golden syrup**
3 heaped Tbsp **smooth peanut butter**
200g (7oz) **porridge oats**
60g (2¼oz) **wheatgerm**
50g (1¾oz) **unsweetened desiccated coconut**
150g (5½oz) **chocolate,** finely chopped or chocolate chips
40g (1½oz) **Rice Krispies®**
40g (1½oz) **sunflower seeds (see tip)**

Preheat the oven to 180°C/350°F/ Gas mark 4.

In a medium-sized bowl stir together the melted butter, brown sugar, golden syrup and peanut butter until smooth. Combine the remaining ingredients together in a separate bowl. Add the peanut butter mixture and mix well until combined.

Press the mixture into a greased 23-cm (9-in) square tin. Bake for 25 minutes, or until the top is golden. Allow to cool then cut into bars.

■ *Chopped nuts can replace the sunflower seeds.*

Nova Scotian seed oatcakes

Wholesome

Oatcakes, traditionally a savoury Scottish biscuit, have evolved into something quite unique on Canada's East Coast. Here is our take on the Nova Scotian oatcake – a version of family friend's Sandra Nowlan's delicious thick, cookie-cake-like recipe combined with a handful of health-giving seeds.

Makes 20–22

450g (1lb) **butter, softened**
200g (7oz) **caster sugar**
300g (10½oz) **plain flour**
150g (5½oz) **wholemeal flour**
¼ tsp **salt**
1 Tbsp **each flax, poppy and sesame seeds,** toasted
2 Tbsp **cold water**
300g (10½oz) **porridge oats**

Preheat the oven to 190°C/375°F/Gas mark 5.

In a large bowl cream the butter and sugar together until smooth. In a separate bowl, sift the flours with the salt. Add to the butter mixture with the toasted seeds and water. Stir to combine.

Lightly flour a work surface and tip the oats on top. Gather the dough into a mound and place on top of the oats. Gently knead the dough into the oats, gathering any oats that scatter away and placing them back into the dough. When the oats are combined, divide the dough into two portions, setting one aside. Shape into a ball and roll into a circle roughly 1.5cm (⅝in) thick. Make sure the circle is of even thickness throughout. Using an 8-cm (3¼-in) wide cookie cutter or drinking glass, cut out oatcakes and place them on an ungreased or parchment-lined baking sheet. Re-shape the extra dough (so it is of similar thickness) and cut oatcakes until all dough is used. Continue with the remaining portion of dough.

Bake for 20–25 minutes, until the edges are just golden but the centres still slightly soft. Allow to cool on the baking sheet for 5 minutes then transfer to wire racks and allow to cool completely.

Nova Scotian seed oatcakes

Pecan and caramel bars

Pecan and caramel bars

Decadent

Let's face it – baking may make you happy, but the accolades received do satisfy our inner show-off needs. This is where these bars come in. And what's better? Pure deliciousness doesn't get much easier.

Makes 20

For the base:
300g (10½oz) **plain flour**
150g (5½oz) **soft brown sugar**
150g (5½oz) **butter,** cut into cubes
200g (7oz) **pecan nuts**

For the topping:
175g (6oz) **butter**
80g (3oz) **soft brown sugar**

Preheat the oven to 180°C/350°F/ Gas mark 4.

To make the base, combine the flour, brown sugar and butter in a large bowl and blend with a fork until crumbly. Pat the mixture into a 23 x 33-cm (9 x13-in) baking tin. Sprinkle the pecan nuts on top and set aside.

Make the topping. In a saucepan combine the butter and brown sugar over medium heat. Bring to the boil and stir constantly for 1 minute. Pour the caramel mixture over the pecan-covered base.

Bake for 18–20 minutes, until the caramel bubbles and the crust is golden. Allow the tin to cool on wire racks before cutting into roughly 4 x 8-cm (1½in x 3¼in) bars.

Store the bars in an airtight container for 3–5 days.

Hello Dolly's

Divine

Who knows why these divine, North American inventions are called Hello Dolly's. Perhaps it's because when the first bite was taken, all the recipient could say was, "Hello Dolly!", they were just that good. And when something is that good, who really cares who Dolly was anyway?

Makes 25 x 1½-in (4-cm) squares

125ml (4fl oz) **butter,** melted
150g (5½oz) **digestive or oatmeal biscuits,** crushed to crumbs
80g (3oz) **unsweetened desiccated coconut**
75g (2¾oz) **pecan nuts,** chopped
150g (5½oz) **chocolate chips or chocolate,** finely chopped
250ml (9fl oz) **sweetened condensed milk**

Preheat the oven to 160°C/325°F/ Gas mark 3.

In a medium-sized bowl combine the melted butter and biscuit crumbs. Pat into a 20 x 20-cm (8 x 8-in) square tin. Cover with coconut, pecan nuts and chocolate. Finish with a drizzled layer of condensed milk.

Bake for 35 minutes, until the edges are golden. Allow to cool, then cut into squares.

Nanaimo bars

Rich

Nanaimo bars are a Canadian favourite. Legend has it that the first recipe was printed in the 1952 Nanaimo Hospital Cookbook, submitted by the Women's Auxiliary of Nanaimo, British Columbia. Thanks go to Aunt Susan's recipe archives for her version of our national staple.

Makes 40 squares

For the base:
220g (7¾oz) butter
2 Tbsp caster sugar
2 eggs, lightly beaten
200g (7oz) unsweetened desiccated coconut
350g (12oz) chocolate biscuits, crushed to crumbs

For the filling:
70g (2½oz) butter, melted
75ml (2½fl oz) milk
1 tsp vanilla extract
500g (1lb 2oz) icing sugar
2 Tbsp instant vanilla pudding powder or custard mix

For the topping:
200g (7oz) plain chocolate
2 Tbsp butter

Preheat the oven to 180°C/350°F/ Gas mark 4. Lightly grease a 23 x 33-cm (9 x 13-in) baking tin.

Combine butter, sugar and eggs in a bowl and whisk until smooth. Add coconut and biscuit crumbs and stir to combine. Press mixture into tin and bake until firm, about 20 minutes. Allow to cool completely on a wire rack.

Combine all the filling ingredients in a mixing bowl and beat until creamy. Spread over the base and chill for 30 minutes in the refrigerator.

For the topping, combing the chocolate and butter in a metal bowl, suspended over a saucepan of simmering water. Stir occasionally until smooth. Spread chocolate misture over the filling and return the tin to the refrigerator to chill until the topping has hardened. The squares will keep in the fridge for up to 7 days.

■ *For a St. Patrick's Day variation (or a treat at any time of the year), add a few drops of peppermint extract and green food colouring to the creamy middle layer and stir until uniform in colour.*

Coconut marshmallows
Delicate

These cloud-like, heavenly marshmallows are more squares than bars, and more sweet treats than cookies, but we've put them in the book due to popular demand. Allow one day of resting time when making these marshmallows.

Makes approx. 40 squares

300g (10½oz) **sweetened desiccated coconut**
4 sachets **unflavoured gelatine** (about 4 Tbsp)
300ml (10fl oz) **water**
600g (1lb 5oz) **caster sugar**
280ml (10fl oz) **golden syrup**
¼ tsp **salt**
1 tsp **coconut extract**

Preheat the oven to 160°C/325°F/ Gas mark 3.

Spread the coconut evenly over a baking sheet and toast in the middle of the oven for about 10 minutes or until golden, stirring halfway through. Allow to cool.

Lightly oil the base and sides of a 28 x 43 x 5-cm (11 x 17 x 2-in) baking dish. Line the dish with foil and then oil the foil. Cover the base of the dish with one third of the toasted coconut. Set aside the remaining coconut in an airtight container.

Combine the gelatine and 150ml (5fl oz) of the water in the bowl of an electric mixer. Combine the sugar, syrup, remaining water and salt in a heavy saucepan. Bring to the boil and cook over high heat until a sugar thermometer inserted reads 116°C/ 240°F (or until a small amount dropped into cold water forms a soft ball when pressed between finger and thumb).

Using the whisk attachment of the electric mixer, whisk the hot syrup very slowly into the gelatine mixture, until the whole mixture is very stiff, about 15 minutes. Beat in the coconut extract. Pour the mixture over the foil-lined, coconut-covered baking dish. Hold the dish with two hands and tap on a worktop to level the surface. Cover with ⅓ of the toasted coconut. Cover with clingfilm and leave to rest at room temperature for 12 hours.

Place the remaining coconut in a large mixing bowl. Turn the marshmallow out on to the a clean work surface. Using a large knife (dipped in water if it gets sticky) cut the marshmallow into 5-cm (2-in) squares. Working in batches, toss the marshmallow squares in the bowl with the remaining coconut, pressing lightly to adhere.

Store in an airtight container at room temperature for 1 week.

Coconut marshmallows

Kids' cookies

Throughout this chapter you will find the results from careful cookie test runs with our discerning panel of pre-teen judges. Children make the best testers. They are honest and their palates are pure. Their comments were harsh at times, but sometimes tough love carves a pathway to success.

Our test products came from our own memories. The cookies we loved, the ones we remembered, the recipes we would equally enjoy as grown-ups. We baked, we made hypotheses, then we presented. What we didn't predict were two basic variables: there had to be colour, interest and preferably a mix of both. A brown blob of what could be pure deliciousness just didn't cut it. Bring on the hundreds and thousands, the jelly fingers, the gorpies studded with sweets. Shards of coconut helped. Sweetness definitely elicited top marks. The most satisfying, then, was the batch of Soft banana-blueberry cookies (page 98). Not much sugar, but a lot of flavour. The little ones loved them. Then again, that panel was under the age of two.

Either way, we've amassed a collection that we hope children around the world will enjoy. If not, it's the panel who is to blame.

Hundreds and thousands biscuits

Rainbow

These were always a favourite of mine right up until my teens. I think it's the lurid pink icing and multi-coloured hundreds and thousands that really appeal to the young (or the young at heart).

Makes 20–24

250g (9oz) **butter,** softened
140g (5oz) **icing sugar,** sifted
1 tsp **vanilla extract**
1 **egg yolk**
375g (13oz) **plain flour**

To decorate:
1 quantity **Coloured icing using pink food colouring (see page 164)**
Hundreds and thousands

Beat the butter, icing sugar, vanilla extract and egg yolk together in a large bowl until creamy. Stir in the flour and mix to a firm dough. Wrap the dough in baking parchment and chill for about 30 minutes.

Preheat the oven to 190°C/375°F/ Gas mark 5.

Line two baking sheets with baking parchment. Roll the dough out to about 5mm (¼in) thick and, using a square cutter, cut out shapes and transfer to the prepared sheets. Bake for 10–12 minutes, or until lightly golden. Transfer to a wire rack and allow to cool completely.

Ice each biscuit with the pink icing and sprinkle with a generous amount of hundreds and thousands, covering the icing completely. Allow to set then store in an airtight container.

Hundreds and thousands biscuits

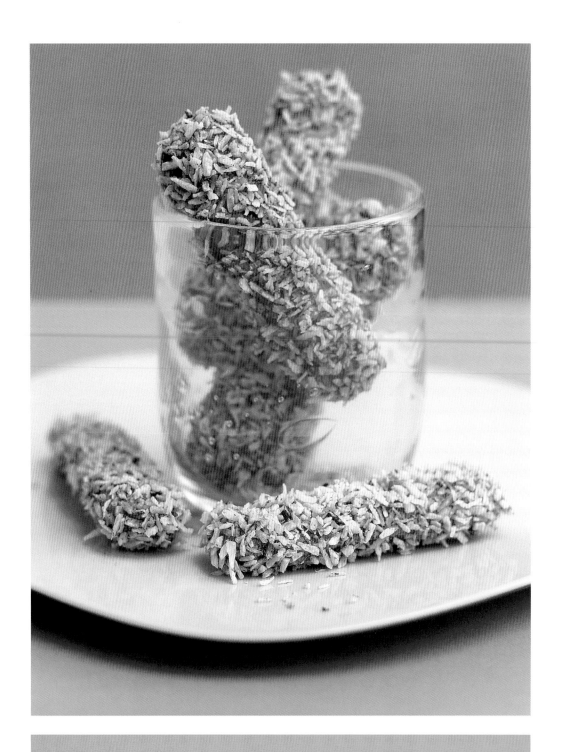

Jelly fingers

Jelly fingers

Simplicity

An easy way to please young partygoers. Make an array of different colours for full effect, using different jelly flavours and food colourings.

Makes 24

25g (1oz) **raspberry jelly crystals**
280g (10oz) **sweetened desiccated coconut**
½ tsp **red food colouring**
24 **bought sponge fingers**

Place the jelly crystals in a large bowl and pour over 300ml (10fl oz) boiling water. Stir to dissolve then cool the jelly until it is of egg white consistency, about 20–30 minutes (keep a close eye on it as it will change quickly).

While the jelly is cooling place the coconut in a large plastic bag, add the food colouring and tie the bag tightly. Rub and shake the coconut in the food colouring until it turns an even pink colour throughout.

One by one dip the sponge fingers into the jelly mixture to coat completely then roll in the coloured coconut. Place on a wire rack to set and continue until all are dipped and coated. Allow them to set for at least 1 hour before serving.

■ *Try using different jelly flavours and food colourings.*

Chocolate peppermint cookies

Minty

Eat them while they are still warm and the oozy peppermint centre will drizzle down your chin. It might be safer to serve them cold to the kids!

Makes 18–20

150g (5½oz) **butter, softened**
150g (5½oz) **caster sugar**
1 **egg yolk**
250g (9oz) **plain flour**
1 tsp **baking powder**
25g (1oz) **cocoa powder**
1 large bar **peppermint-filled chocolate**
1 quantity **Coloured icing using green food colouring (see page 164)**

Preheat the oven to 190°C/375°F/ Gas mark 5. Line two baking sheets with baking parchment.

Beat the butter and sugar together in a large bowl until pale and creamy. Add the egg yolk and mix to combine. In a separate bowl sift the flour, baking powder and cocoa powder. Stir the dry ingredients into the butter and mix well to form a stiff dough.

Roll out about one third of the mixture to about 2–3mm (⅟₁₆–⅛in) thick and, using a 5– 5.5-cm (2–2¼-in) round cutter, cut out as many rounds as possible. Using a palette knife, transfer the rounds on to the baking sheets, leaving a little space between them to allow for spreading. Place one square of chocolate in the centre of each round. Roll out the remaining dough to the same thickness and cut larger rounds using a 7–7.5-cm (2¾–3-in) round cutter. Place the larger rounds over the chocolate-topped rounds and seal well around the edges. Don't worry if the tops crack a little.

Bake the cookies for about 10 minutes then allow to cool on the baking sheet for a further 5 minutes. Transfer to a wire rack and allow to cool completely before making the green icing.

Drizzle the icing over the cookies in a zig-zag pattern and leave to set.

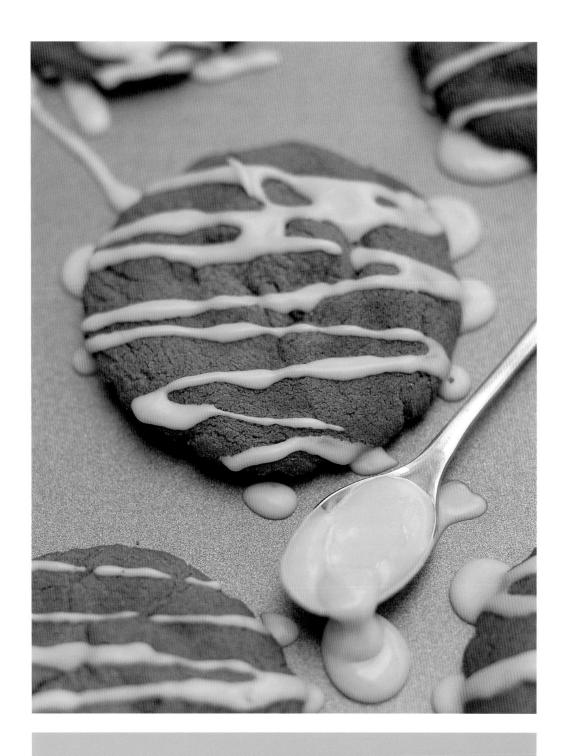

Chocolate peppermint cookies

Hokey pokey biscuits

Toffee-flavoured

Hokey pokey are crunchy pieces of toffee that are immersed in vanilla ice cream. This ice cream is a New Zealand icon that is second only to plain vanilla. These biscuits have similar crunchy toffee characteristics and they are great with a large glass of milk.

Makes 20–24

125g (4½oz) **butter,** softened
150g (5½oz) **caster sugar**
1 Tbsp **milk**
1 Tbsp **golden syrup**
1 tsp **bicarbonate of soda**
225g (8oz) **plain flour**

Preheat the oven to 180°C/350°F/ Gas mark 4. Line a baking sheet with baking parchment.

Put the butter, sugar, milk and golden syrup in a saucepan and melt gently until almost boiling. Remove from the heat and cool for about 15–20 minutes. Combine with the bicarbonate of soda and flour and stir into the butter mixture.

Working quickly, roll the mixture into tablespoon-sized balls and place on the baking sheet. Press down with a fork and bake for 15–18 minutes, or until golden.

■ *Add 2 tsp ground ginger to make ginger cookies.*

Peanut brownie cookies

Nutty

Traditionally, in my family, these have always been made with peanuts still in their skins. I know some people prefer them without so I'll leave it up to you.

Makes 24

125g (4½oz) **butter, softened**
200g (7oz) **caster sugar**
1 **egg,** lightly beaten
225g (8oz) **plain flour**
1 tsp **baking powder**
1 pinch **salt**
3 Tbsp **cocoa powder**
200g (7oz) **unsalted peanuts,**
 in their skins, or without (optional)

Preheat the oven to 180°C/350°F/Gas mark 4. Line a large baking sheet with baking parchment.

Cream the butter and sugar until pale. Add the egg and beat to combine. In a separate bowl combine the flour, baking powder, salt and cocoa powder and add to the creamed mixture. Combine until a stiff mixture forms then stir in the peanuts until evenly dispersed.

Roll the mixture into heaped tablespoon-sized balls and place on the baking sheet, leaving a little space between them to allow for spreading.

Bake for 14–16 minutes, or until firm to the touch. Remove from the oven, transfer to a wire rack and allow to cool completely.

Lolly cake

Lolly cake

Sweet

It may only be New Zealanders who know what lolly cake is so here is my chance to share this childhood memory with the world.

Makes 1 log

100g (3½oz) **butter,** melted
250g (9oz) **malted milk biscuits,** crushed
200ml (7fl oz) **sweetened condensed milk**
200g (7oz) **foam fruit sweets**
30g (1oz) **sweetened desiccated coconut**

Combine the melted butter, biscuits, condensed milk and sweets in a large bowl and mix to combine.

On a large, flat surface lay out a piece of baking parchment about 45cm (18in) long. Put the biscuit mixture on to the paper and manipulate it into a log shape about 25cm (10in) long. Roll up the paper and tighten the log so it stretches to about 30cm (12in) long. Open the paper again and sprinkle over the coconut. Roll the log in the coconut until evenly coated then roll up tightly in the baking parchment. Tear off a large piece of foil and place the log on the foil. Roll up tightly, securing the ends, then refrigerate overnight or until firm.

Unwrap the log and slice into pieces to serve.

Peanut butter cookies

Comforting

These meltingly soft peanut butter concoctions, punctuated by crunchy nuts, will put a smile on all faces, young and old.

Makes 38–40

110g (4oz) **butter,** softened
100g (3½oz) **caster sugar**
80g (3oz) **light brown sugar**
1 **egg,** lightly beaten
220g (8oz) **smooth peanut butter**
300g (10½oz) **plain flour**
½ tsp **salt**
1 tsp **bicarbonate of soda**
80g (3oz) **chopped peanuts**
  or walnuts, toasted

Preheat the oven to 180°C/350°F/ Gas mark 4.

In a large mixing bowl cream the butter and sugars until smooth. Beat in the egg and peanut butter and continue to beat until combined. In a separate bowl, sift the flour, salt and bicarbonate of soda together. Add to the peanut butter mixture and stir just until combined. Stir in the toasted nuts.

Drop rounded teaspoonfuls of the mixture on to the baking sheet and depress the balls lightly with the prongs of a fork. Bake for 8–10 minutes, until just cooked through. Allow to cool for 5 minutes on the baking sheet then transfer to wire racks and allow to cool completely.

■ *For added smiles, add 100g (3½oz) chopped chocolate to the cookie dough when you add the chopped nuts.*

Ranger cookies

Chewy

This favourite family recipe is as much of a hit with the grown-ups as it is with the kids. The distinctive texture comes from the cornflakes, which add crunch, the coconut, which adds texture and the dates, which add moisture and sweetness.

Makes approx. 50

220g (8oz) **butter**
180g (6oz) **caster sugar**
220g (8oz) **brown sugar**
2 **eggs**
200g (7oz) **sweetened desiccated coconut**
275g (9¾oz) **dates,** finely chopped
375g (13oz) **plain flour**
1 tsp **baking powder**
160g (5½oz) **cornflakes**

Preheat the oven to 180°C/350°F/ Gas mark 4.

Cream the butter and sugars until light and fluffy. Add the eggs, one at a time, beating until smooth. Stir in the coconut and dates. Sift the flour and baking powder together and stir into batter. Work the cornflakes into the batter (it is easiest to use your hands for this) until roughly combined.

Form into rounded tablespoon-sized balls and place on ungreased baking sheets 5cm (2in) apart. Bake for 15 minutes, or until lightly golden. Allow to cool on the baking sheets for 5 minutes then transfer to wire racks and allow to cool completely.

Gingerbread men

Easy-going

It's hard to find a gingerbread men recipe that is both easy to roll and decorate and delicious to eat. Well, here it is, straight from the Jamieson family kitchen, where the queens of cookie decorating reside. Play with cookie cutters – this recipe isn't exclusive to men!

The yield depends on the size of cutter used. If you use 9-cm (3½-in) cutters you will have 7 gingerbread men.

150g (5½oz) **butter**
130g (4½oz) **caster sugar**
1 **egg**
200ml (7fl oz) **treacle or molasses**
450g (1lb) **plain flour**
½ tsp **baking powder**
1 tsp **bicarbonate of soda**
1 tsp **salt**
1 tsp **ground ginger**
½ tsp **ground cloves**
½ tsp **ground cinnamon**

Suggested decorations:
Royal eggnog icing (see page 164)
Silver balls
Chocolate drops
Hundreds and thousands

Combine the butter and sugar in a large bowl and beat, using an electric mixer, until light and fluffy. Add the egg and treacle and beat until smooth. In a separate bowl, sift the flour with the baking powder, soda, salt, cinnamon and cloves. Slowly add the flour mixture to the treacle mixture in three separate stages, stirring with a wooden spoon until combined.

Divide the dough into four balls, flatten and wrap in clingfilm then refrigerate for at least 1 hour before use.

Preheat the oven to 190°C/375°F/ Gas mark 5.

Roll the balls, one at a time, between two sheets of greaseproof paper to a 3-mm (⅛-in) thickness. Peel off the top layer and cut into patterns. Carefully transfer cut-outs to ungreased baking trays. Bake for 10–15 minutes, until just cooked. Do not over-cook. Allow the gingerbread men to cool on trays, for 5 minutes, then transfer to racks and allow to cool completely. Decorate as you wish.

■ *The recipe can easily be doubled, or made in advance. Wrap dough in cling-film and freeze for up to 1 month. Allow to thaw in the fridge overnight before using.*

Gingerbread men

Great gorpies

Universal

"Gorp" is the great energy booster mix made of peanuts, raisins and chocolate chips. It is eaten in handfuls, and here is also added in handfuls. All right, my kids' panel has revised gorp to include simply M&M's® and peanuts. Raisins are also a welcome addition. This recipe is egg-free.

Makes 32

220g (8oz) **butter, softened**
200g (7oz) **brown sugar**
2 grown-up handfuls **peanuts**
    (about 100g/3½oz)
2 grown-up handfuls **M&M's®**
    (about 100g/3½oz)
140g (5oz) **wholemeal flour**
140g (5oz) **plain flour**
1 tsp **bicarbonate of soda**
2 tsp **milk**

Preheat the oven to 180°C/350°F/ Gas mark 4. Grease or line two baking sheets with baking parchment.

Beat the butter and sugar together until smooth. Stir in the peanuts and M&M's®. Sift the flours together with the bicarbonate of soda and add to the butter mixture. Add the milk and stir to combine. Shape the dough into rounded tablespoonfuls with your hands and drop the mounds on to greased or parchment-lined baking sheets.

Bake for 10–12 minutes, just until set. Allow to cool on the baking sheets for 5 minutes then transfer to wire racks and allow to cool completely.

Oatmeal raisin cookies

Warming

Our version of this classic cookie is very chewy, is packed with oats and raisins, and features a lovely hint of cinnamon.

Makes 35

165g (6oz) **butter, softened**
150g (5½oz) **brown sugar**
110g (4oz) **caster sugar**
1 **egg**
2 Tbsp **water**
2 tsp **vanilla extract**
120g (4½oz) **plain flour**
⅛ tsp **salt**
1 tsp **bicarbonate of soda**
1 tsp **ground cinnamon**
300g (10½oz) **porridge oats**
220g (8oz) **raisins**

Preheat the oven to 180°C/350°F/ Gas mark 4.

Beat the butter and sugars in an electric mixer until light and fluffy. Beat in the egg, water and vanilla extract until combined. In a separate bowl, sift together the flour, salt, bicarbonate of soda and cinnamon. Add to the butter mixture along with the oats and raisins, stirring just until combined.

Roll the dough into tablespoon-sized balls with your hands and place 5cm (2in) apart on ungreased baking sheets. Bake for 12–14 minutes, until the edges are crispy but the centres are soft and bubbling. Remove from the oven and allow to cool on the baking sheets for 5 minutes. Don't over-bake – the cookies will continue to cook on the sheets. Transfer to wire racks and allow to cool completely.

Store the cookies in an airtight container for 3–5 days, or freeze for up to 2 months.

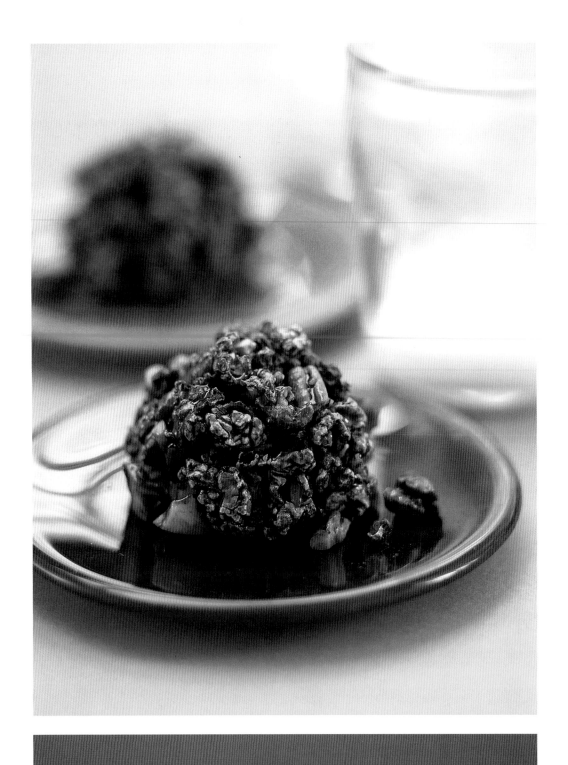

Popcorn balls

Popcorn balls

Sticky

Thanks once again to Aunt Sandra for these delectable balls. They are chewy, not at all dry, and for all the Americans out there, incredibly similar in flavour to Cracker Jacks.

Makes 10–14

70g (2½oz) **popped popcorn**
250ml (9fl oz) **molasses (see tip)**
150g (5½oz) **caster sugar**
2 Tbsp **white vinegar**
2 Tbsp **butter**
125ml (4½fl oz) **water**
½ tsp **bicarbonate of soda**
200g (7oz) **pecans or walnuts,**
    chopped (or a combination of both)

Put the popped popcorn into two large, separate bowls (this will make combining with the molasses syrup a much easier task). Set aside.

Combine the molasses, sugar, white vinegar, butter and water in a saucepan over medium heat. Boil gently, without stirring, until the mixture begins to bubble and a sugar thermometer inserted reads 116°C/240°F (or until a small amount dropped into cold water forms a soft ball when pressed between finger and thumb). Stir in the bicarbonate of soda. Working quickly, pour the syrup over the two bowls of popcorn. Add the chopped nuts and stir to combine.

When the popcorn is cool enough to handle, butter your hands, scoop up the popcorn by the fistful and roll into balls. Wrap each ball individually in clingfilm.

◼ *Try to seek out molasses rather than using treacle in this recipe. Treacle will work, but molasses lends more of a caramel flavour.*

Hundreds and thousands ice cream sandwiches

Colourful

Hundreds and thousands, commonly yet boringly called "sprinkles" in North America, are enough to make any child smile. Sprinkled over a cookie and sandwiched around creamy ice cream makes for sheer bliss!

Makes 10–15

1 quantity **Hundreds and thousands biscuits (see page 78)**
1L (1¾pt) **strawberry (or any favourite) ice cream,** slightly softened
Extra hundreds and thousands, for decorating

Place half the biscuits, hundreds and thousands-side down, on a work surface. Spoon softened strawberry ice cream about 2cm (1in) thick on the underside of each biscuit. Place a matching biscuit on top of the ice cream, top-side facing up. Sprinkle the exposed ice cream with more hundreds and thousands.

Place the sandwich in an airtight container and immediately transfer to the freezer to harden completely. Repeat with the remaining ice cream and biscuits. Store the sandwiches in airtight container in the freezer for 3–4 days.

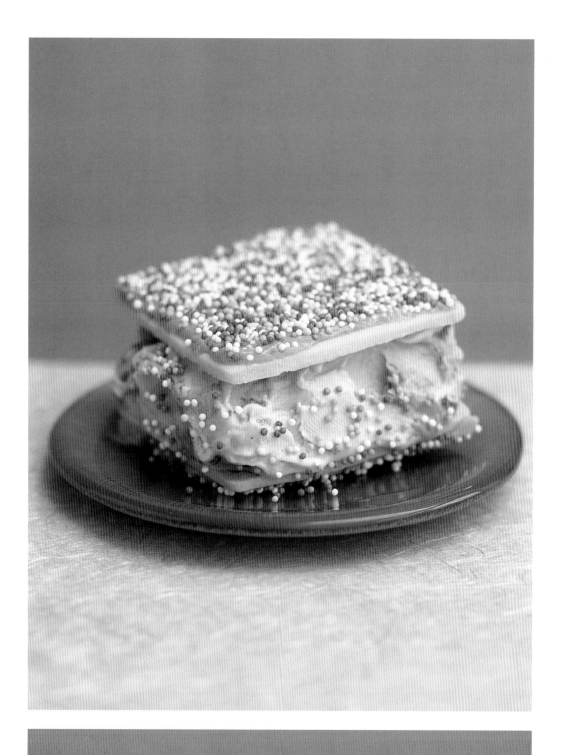

Hundreds and thousands ice cream sandwiches

Soft banana-blueberry cookies

Flavoursome

Baby and mum play dates are great for sharing recipes, and these cookies passed the toddler test with flying colours. Substitute blueberries for other berries, if you prefer, or use finely chopped raisins or cranberries.

Makes 30-32

1 **ripe medium banana,** mashed
75g (2¾oz) **butter (see tip),** softened
40g (1½oz) **brown sugar**
75ml (2½fl oz) **apple juice**
1 **egg**
½ tsp **vanilla extract**
75g (2¾oz) **plain flour**
½ tsp **bicarbonate of soda**
50g (1¾oz) **porridge oats**
75g (2¾oz) **blueberries,** fresh
   or frozen

Preheat the oven to 180°C/350°F/ Gas mark 4. Lightly grease a baking sheet or line it with baking parchment.

Combine the mashed banana, butter and brown sugar in a mixing bowl and stir until combined. Add apple juice, egg and vanilla, and stir until smooth. In a separate bowl, sift the flour with the bicarbonate of soda. Add to the banana mixture along with the oats. Carefully add the blueberries – too much stirring at this point will turn the batter blue!

Drop the batter by the teaspoonful on to the prepared baking sheet, spacing the mounds about 5cm (2in) apart. Bake for 10 minutes, until set. Allow to cool on the baking sheet for 5 minutes then transfer to wire racks and allow to cool completely. Store the cookies in an airtight container for up to 5 days, or freeze for up to 2 months.

■ *You can substitute soy or peanut butter for the butter if you prefer.*

Witchy fingers

Creepy

Thanks to Diane Nichols for sharing the recipe for these tasty, yet very eerie, Halloween fingers.

Makes approx. 26–28

220g (7¾oz) **butter**
125g (4½oz) **icing sugar**
1 **egg**
1 tsp **almond extract**
1 tsp **vanilla extract**
425–450g (15oz–1lb) **plain flour**
1 tsp **baking powder**
1 tsp **salt**
About 30 **flaked almonds**
Red decorating gel (optional)

Preheat the oven to 180°C/350°F/ Gas mark 4. Line two baking sheets with baking parchment.

Cream the butter and icing sugar in an electric mixer until light and fluffy. Add the egg together with the almond and vanilla extracts and beat until smooth. In a separate bowl, sift the flour with the baking powder and salt. Add to the butter mixture and stir to combine.

Add a little more flour if the dough feels sticky.

Roll the dough into tablespoon-sized balls then form into index finger-shaped logs and place on baking sheets. Flatten slightly at the knuckles and make little wrinkle lines with the tip of a knife. Put a drop of red decorating gel at the tip of each finger, if using, and stick a flaked almond over to form a fingernail. Don't worry if the almonds are cracked – that only adds to the creepiness of the fingers!

Bake for 12–15 minutes, until the fingers are golden and cooked through. Allow to cool on the baking sheets then transfer to wire racks to cool completely.

Store in airtight containers for 3–5 days, or freeze for up to 2 months.

Coffee-time cookies

Coffee. Tea. Cookies. What does this mean to you?

To my grandmother, it's a gathering of women from her church group. Grammy will serve something with ginger, something lacy, and something with a touch of jam. The ladies will carefully perch on sofas and chairs, teacups in one hand, a cookie in the other, a pretty napkin placed on their laps. Bites will be savoured, but over-eating is out of the question.

To others it could be an afternoon on the beach, when the barbecue is dying down. People sit around the fire, drinking tea and eating freshly baked cookies from a tin. With toes nestled in the sand they take a sip, take a bite, take another sip. One cup is never enough, nor is one cookie.

Or how about the morning-coffee party, the ones where good friends gather to lounge on overstuffed sofas. The aroma of freshly ground coffee emanates from the kitchen and stories are flowing. Chocolate is necessary here, or perhaps a touch of espresso-studded shortbread.

To everyone, however, it all boils down to a few basic needs: friendship, hot drinks and cookies.

Biscotti

Biscotti
Traditional

Biscotti is the plural of biscotto, which literally means "twice baked" in Italian. This method of baking produces a very hard, crunchy biscuit, which is delicious dunked in vin santo (Tuscan dessert wine) or served with a cup of coffee.

Makes approx. 30

250g (9oz) **plain flour**
150g (5½oz) **caster sugar**
1 tsp **baking powder**
100g (3½oz) **crystallized ginger,**
   cut into chunks
125g (4½oz) **Brazil nuts,** chopped
   into chunks
3 **eggs**

Variation:
Omit the crystallized ginger and
   Brazil nuts and add:
200g (7oz) **whole almonds,** blanched
150g (5½oz) **plain chocolate,** cut into
   chunks
Or:
150g (5½oz) **pistachio nuts**
150g (5½oz) **plain chocolate,** cut into
   chunks

Preheat the oven to 180°C/350°F/ Gas mark 4. Line two large baking sheets with baking parchment and set aside.

Put all the dry ingredients in a large bowl and mix to combine. Add the eggs and stir until the mixture comes together in a ball, adding a little extra flour if it is too wet. Halve the mixture and place each half on the baking parchment. Shape into long, flat log shapes about 25cm (10in) long, 10cm (4in) wide and 2.5cm (1in) high. Bake for about 20 minutes, or until the logs are cooked through and only very lightly golden.

Remove from the oven and, when they are cool enough to handle, lift the logs on to a board, and slice thinly (about 7mm/⅜in thick) on the diagonal, then place the separate biscuits back flat on the baking sheets. Bake for 10 minutes then turn and bake for a further 5 minutes on the other side or until lightly golden and crispy. Transfer to a wire rack and allow to cool completely.

These will keep in an airtight container for about 7–10 days.

Berry chocolate florentines

Decadent

These large flat biscuits are usually made with candied peel and glacé cherries instead of the mixed dried berries. Chocolate-coated or not, they are simply divine!

Makes 12

75g (2¾oz) **butter**
75g (2¾oz) **light brown sugar**
50g (1¾oz) **plain flour**
50g (1¾oz) **flaked almonds**, toasted
100g (3½oz) **mixed dried berries, e.g. cranberries, blueberries, cherries, strawberries**
150g (5½oz) **plain chocolate, chopped**
¼–½ tsp **ground mixed spice**

Preheat the oven to 180°C/350°F/ Gas mark 4. Line a large baking sheet with baking parchment.

Heat the butter and sugar together in a saucepan until the sugar dissolves and they bind together. Remove from the heat and mix in the flour, then add the nuts and berries.

Put tablespoonfuls full of the mixture, quite widely spaced, on the baking sheet and flatten slightly using the back of the spoon. You may need to bake them in two batches.

Bake the Florentines for 10–12 minutes, or until spread flat and golden. While still hot, neaten up the edges using a knife and allow to cool completely on the baking sheet. Melt the chocolate over a saucepan of simmering water or in the microwave. Stir in the mixed spice and mix well. Using a palette knife, spread the chocolate over the flat side of the Florentines and allow to cool before serving.

Berry chocolate florentines

Ricciarelli

Delicate

These little diamond-shaped biscuits make the perfect gift.

Makes 24

200g (7oz) **ground almonds**
200g (7oz) **icing sugar**, sifted
1 Tbsp **plain flour**
½ tsp **baking powder**
2 **egg whites**
1 tsp **amaretto or rum**
Grated rind of 1 **orange**
50g (1¾oz) **icing sugar**, sifted,
   for rolling

Preheat the oven to 140°C/275°F/ Gas mark 1. Line two baking sheets with baking parchment.

Combine the ground almonds, sifted icing sugar, flour and baking powder in a large bowl. Mix well to combine. In a separate bowl beat the egg whites until stiff peaks form. Mix the egg whites into the almond mixture, along with the amaretto and orange rind.

Place the extra icing sugar in a separate shallow bowl. Form the mixture into heaped teaspoon-sized balls and roll them in the extra icing sugar. Form each ball into a diamond shape, using the palm of your hand to flatten them and your fingers to pinch in the sides.

Bake for 25–30 minutes, or until firm and lightly golden.

Gingernuts

Crunchy

These are the perfect balance between crunchy and chewy. I put them to the test on Lottie Davies and Tom Norrington-Davies, photographer and food writer respectively. They passed with flying colours, as a further four were consumed over breakfast – what more can I say!

Makes 16

60g (2¼oz) **butter**
1 Tbsp **stem ginger syrup**
100ml (3½fl oz) **golden syrup**
1 tsp **bicarbonate of soda**
50g (1¾oz) **stem ginger (about 2 pieces)**, finely chopped
200g (7oz) **plain flour**
100g (3½oz) **light brown sugar**

Preheat the oven to 160°C/325°F/ Gas mark 3. Line two baking sheets with baking parchment.

Place the butter, ginger syrup and golden syrup in a saucepan and stir over low heat until the butter has melted. Add the bicarbonate of soda and allow it to foam. Remove from the heat, stir in the stem ginger and set aside.

Put the flour and sugar in a large mixing bowl and mix to combine. Add the butter mixture and stir well. Roll heaped tablespoons of the mixture into balls and place them on the baking sheet, leaving enough space to allow for spreading.

Bake for 18–20 minutes, or until firm. Leave on the baking sheet for a few minutes then transfer to a wire rack and allow to cool completely.

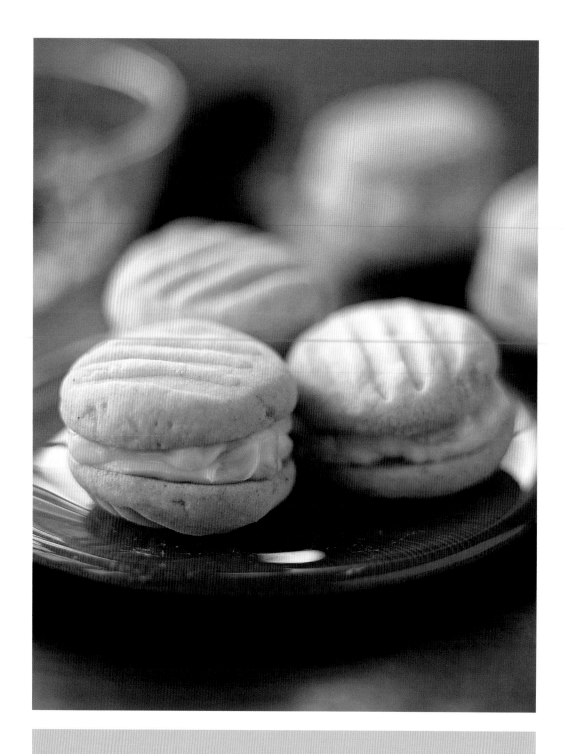

Ginger kisses

Ginger kisses

Melt-in-the-mouth

Filled with a delicately sweet ginger cream, these are definitely the ones to impress the in-laws with!

Makes 20–24

250g (9oz) **butter**, softened
115g (4¼oz) **icing sugar**, sieved
1 **egg**, lightly beaten
3 tsp **ground ginger**
225g (8oz) **plain flour**
150g (5½oz) **cornflour**

For the filling:
250g (9oz) **mascarpone**
50g (1¾oz) **stem ginger**, finely chopped
1 Tbsp **stem ginger syrup**
50g (1¾oz) **demerara sugar**
½ tsp **vanilla extract**

Preheat the oven to 170°C/325°F/Gas mark 3. Line two baking sheets with baking parchment.

In a large bowl beat the butter until pale and creamy. Gradually add the icing sugar, beating well after each addition until the mixture is light and fluffy. Beat in the egg until well combined. If the mixture starts to curdle, add a tablespoon of the flour. In a separate bowl combine the ginger, flour and cornflour. Sift the dry ingredients into the butter mixture and mix thoroughly. Roll teaspoon-sized amounts into balls and press down with a fork.

Bake for 20–22 minutes, or until firm and lightly golden in colour. Transfer to a wire rack and allow to cool completely.

While the biscuits are cooling prepare the filling. Combine all the ingredients in a bowl and set aside. When the biscuits are cool enough spread the filling on half the biscuits then place the remaining biscuits on top.

Bumblebees

Nostalgic

Bumblebees are a real childhood memory. Mum used to make them for every school gala or fair. They last for ages and are also a great Christmas time standby.

Makes 30–36

150g (5½oz) **dates**
150g (5½oz) **sultanas**
125g (4½oz) **walnuts**
50g (1¾oz) **stem ginger,** roughly chopped
100g (3½oz) **dried figs (about** 6–8**)**
375ml (13fl oz) **sweetened condensed milk**
100g (3½oz) **sweetened desiccated coconut,** plus extra for coating

Preheat the oven to 160°C/325°F/ Gas mark 3. Line a large baking sheet with baking parchment.

Put the dates, sultanas, walnuts, stem ginger and figs in a food processor and pulse to a coarse mince. Transfer the mixture to a large bowl and add the condensed milk and coconut. Stir well to combine. Roll the mixture into tablespoon-sized balls and coat in extra coconut then place on the lined baking sheet. Repeat until all the mixture is used up.

Bake for 25–30 minutes, or until lightly golden.

These can be stored in an airtight container for up to 1 month.

Espresso shortbread slice

Sophisticated

Whether cut into thin or thick slices, these delicious shortbreads are bound to perk up any coffee moment.

Makes 6 x 10-cm (4-in) tartlets
or 2 x 20-cm (8-in) tarts

220g (8oz) **butter**
200g (7oz) **caster sugar**
1 **egg yolk**
2 tsp **vanilla extract**
300g (10½oz) **plain flour**
1½ tsp **baking powder**
2 Tbsp **espresso coffee beans,**
finely ground

For the topping:
150g (5½oz) **plain chocolate**
1 Tbsp **cold coffee**
1 Tbsp **butter**

Preheat the oven to 180°C/350°F/ Gas mark 4. Lightly grease six 10-cm tartlet tins or two 20-cm (8-in) flan tins.

Using an electric mixer, beat the butter and sugar until light and fluffy. Add the egg yolk and vanilla extract and beat until combined. In a separate bowl sift together the flour and baking powder. Stir in the ground espresso beans.

Add the flour mixture to the butter mixture and stir briefly, then tip the mixture on to a lightly floured board and knead together with your hands until combined.

Divide the dough into six (or two) equal parts and pat the dough into your chosen tart tins. Bake for 20 minutes, until golden. Transfer the tins to wire racks and allow to cool completely.

While the shortbread is cooling, make the topping. Melt the chocolate in a double boiler. As it melts, add the coffee and butter and stir to combine. If the chocolate is quite thick once melted, add a little more coffee. Using the prongs of a fork, drizzle the melted chocolate over the shortbread. (Flick with your wrist – making a bit of a mess is mandatory!).

Allow to cool completely before removing the shortbread from the tins. Slice and serve. Store the remaining shortbread in an airtight container for up to 3 days.

Raspberry Shrewsburys

Irresistibly sweet

I had always known of these biscuits as Raspberry Shrewsburys until I came to England. After making them at the photo shoot and hearing everyone call them Jammy dodgers I simply had to convert. Buttery biscuits sandwiched together with raspberry jam, these are good at coffee time and also make a lunch box treat.

Makes 20

250g (9oz) **flour**
175g (6oz) **butter**
125g (4½oz) **caster sugar**
1 large **egg yolk**
200g (7oz) **raspberry jam**
Juice of 1 **lemon**

Put the flour and butter in a food processor and process until the mixture resembles breadcrumbs. Add the sugar and egg yolk and process until the mixture starts to form a dough. Alternatively, cut the butter into small cubes and add to the flour. Using your fingers, rub the butter into the flour until it makes fine breadcrumbs. Add the sugar and egg yolks and mix to a smooth dough.

On a lightly floured surface knead the dough until it comes together. Shape into a ball and wrap in baking parchment and chill for at least 30 minutes.

Preheat the oven to 170°C/325°F/ Gas mark 3. Line a baking sheet with baking parchment.

Roll out the dough on a lightly floured surface to about 3mm (⅛in) thick and cut out rounds using a 5–6-cm (2–2½-in) crimped cutter. Re-roll the trimmings and cut out more rounds until you have 40. Use a 1-cm (½-in) piping nozzle to remove the centre from 20 of the rounds.

Bake for 10–12 minutes, or until lightly golden in colour. Remove from the oven and allow to cool for a few minutes on the baking sheet then transfer to a wire rack and allow to cool completely.

While the biscuits are cooling, put the jam and lemon juice in a saucepan and heat to a simmer. Spoon or brush the jam over the base of a whole round and sandwich with a round with its centre removed on top. Continue until all are done. Allow to cool completely.

Raspberry Shrewsburys

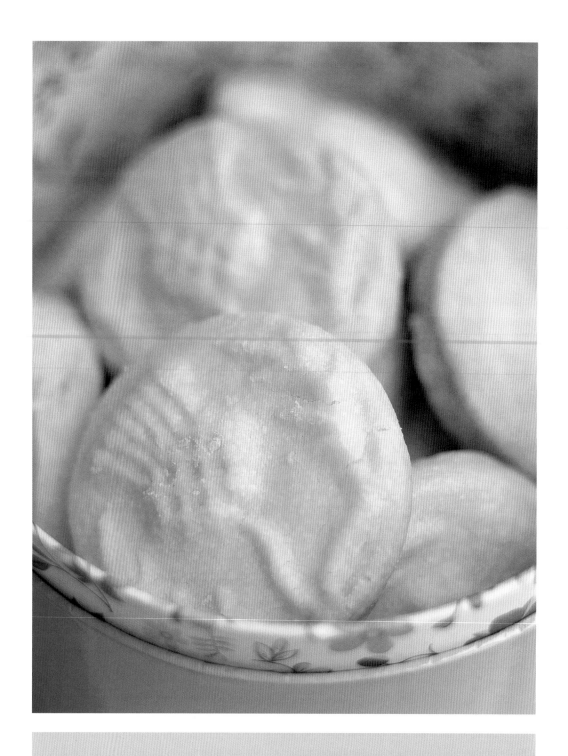

Classic shortbread

Classic shortbread

Angelic

This recipe comes from Elizabeth Green, who used to run a café and bakery in Halifax, Nova Scotia. The recipe is from her Great Aunt Josie, who came from Prince Edward Island. It is the best shortbread I've ever tasted and, in the words of my brother-in-law, they taste as if they've been "kissed by an angel".

Makes 40 x 5-cm (2-in) diameter cookies

50g (1¾oz) **icing sugar,** sifted
450g (1lb) **butter,** softened
1 tsp **vanilla extract**
60g (2¼oz) **cornflour,** sifted
525g (1lb 3oz) **plain flour,** sifted

Preheat the oven to 180°C/350°F/ Gas mark 4.

Combine the sifted icing sugar and butter in a large mixing bowl and beat until very light and fluffy. Add the vanilla extract and beat until smooth. In a separate bowl, combine the sifted flour and cornflour. Using a wooden spoon, stir the flour mixture into the butter mixture and work together until combined.

Divide the dough into two equal mounds. Flour a work surface and roll the first mound into a 24-cm (9 ½-in) wide circle, almost 1.5cm (⅝in) thick. Cut the dough into desired shapes and place on parchment-lined baking sheets. (We used a 5-cm (2-in) wide round wooden thistle mould, but you can use an ordinary round cutter.)

Bake for 15–20 minutes, until slightly golden. Allow to cool for 5 minutes then transfer to wire racks and allow to cool completely.

Meanwhile, continue baking the remaining shortbread. Top the shortbread, if liked, with a swirl of Vanilla butter icing (see page 166).

Almond and quince thumbprints

Comforting

Thumbprints are a comforting, jam-centred, old-fashioned cookie. Here they take on a slightly modern twist with the addition of quince jelly. However, any jelly or jam will do.

Makes 30

110g (3½oz) **caster sugar**
220g (8oz) **butter**, softened
60g (2¼oz) **icing sugar**
150g (5½oz) **whole almonds,**
   blanched, toasted and ground
   to a fine powder
1 **egg yolk**
1 tsp **vanilla extract**
½ tsp **almond essence**
300g (10½oz) **plain flour**
½ tsp **baking powder**
¼ tsp **salt**
125g (4½oz) **quince jelly**

Preheat the oven to 180°C/350°F/Gas mark 4.

Using an electric mixer, beat the sugar and butter until light and fluffy. Beat in the icing sugar, ground almonds, egg yolk, vanilla extract and almond essence. In a separate bowl, sift together the flour, baking powder and salt. Add to the butter mixture and stir just until combined.

Shape rounded teaspoonfuls of the dough into balls and place on ungreased baking sheets about 5cm (2in) apart. Make an indentation in the centre of each ball with your thumb, or with the end of a wooden spoon. Fill the indentations with ¼ tsp quince jelly. Bake for 12 minutes, or until the cookies are golden. Cool on the baking sheets for 5 minutes, then transfer to wire racks and allow to cool completely.

Almond and quince thumbprints

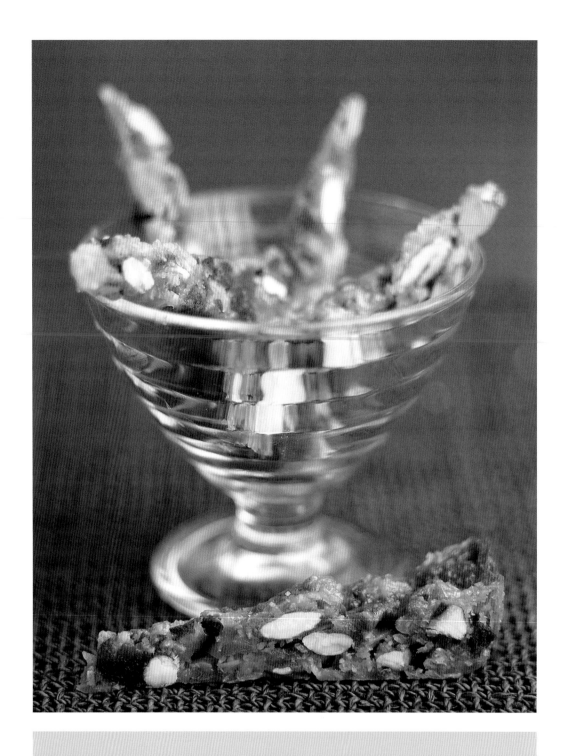

Panforte

Panforte

Reminiscent

Panforte, a speciality from the Italian city of Siena, means "strong bread". We prefer to think of it as "beautiful, edible, sweet stained glass", but that's too wordy. Our version features very untraditional pistachio nuts, apricots and ground cardamom for a touch of Middle Eastern flair.

Makes 1 x 23-cm (9-in) cake

100g (3½oz) **shelled pistachio nuts**
100g (3½oz) **almonds**
100g (3½oz) **dried apricots,** roughly chopped
100g (3½oz) **candied peel,** roughly chopped
50g (1¾oz) **sweetened desiccated coconut**
Grated rind of 1 **lemon**
1 tsp **ground cardamom**
75g (2¾oz) **plain flour**
150g (5½oz) **caster sugar**
4 Tbsp **honey**
50g (1¾oz) **butter**
Icing sugar, for dusting (optional)

Preheat the oven to 150°C/300°F/ Gas mark 2.

Line a 23-cm (9-in) spring-release tin with baking parchment or rice paper. Toast the nuts in a frying pan over medium heat, stirring occasionally until golden. Allow to cool. Place the toasted nuts in a large bowl and toss with the apricots, candied peel, coconut, lemon rind, cardamom and flour.

Combine the sugar, honey and butter in a saucepan over medium heat. Cook, stirring occasionally, until the mixture begins to bubble and a sugar thermometer inserted reads 116°C/ 240°F (or until a small amount dropped into cold water forms a soft ball when pressed between finger and thumb).

Pour the syrup into the nut mixture and quickly combine – it will stiffen quickly. If cool enough, use your hands to blend. Pat the mixture into the tin, press down the surface evenly and bake for 35 minutes. It will not change visually during cooking, but don't worry!

Allow to cool for 30 minutes, then run a knife around the edge. Remove the paper from beneath the panforte, then leave to cool completely. Dust heavily with icing sugar, if liked. Store in an airtight container, or thinly slice and serve.

Dessert-time cookies

I've done drastic things to satisfy my cookie cravings. I've faced the kind of adversity that would force the average person to throw in the kitchen towel. But once a craving strikes, nothing has ever stood in my way. I have found myself in ill-equipped kitchens baking cookies in a roasting tin, in microwave ovens and in a frying pan over an open fire. I've even made little cookies in the bottoms of muffin tins.

But I've learned my lesson. I now travel with my beloved baking sheet and plenty of baking parchment in my overnight bag so I can make cookies with ease and grace whenever I want.

Many cookies don't require a sophisticated kit. But there are some – the dainty, dessert-worthy kind – that are more likely to maintain their delicate status when made with the right equipment. Persian lace cookies (page 132) slip from the tin. Langues de chat (page 123) emerge evenly golden. Bark (page 137) bubbles uniformly under the heat.

Experience proves that any cookie is welcome for dessert, and this selection will provide all you need to round off a meal in style. People might raise an eyebrow, until, that is, they sample your cookies.

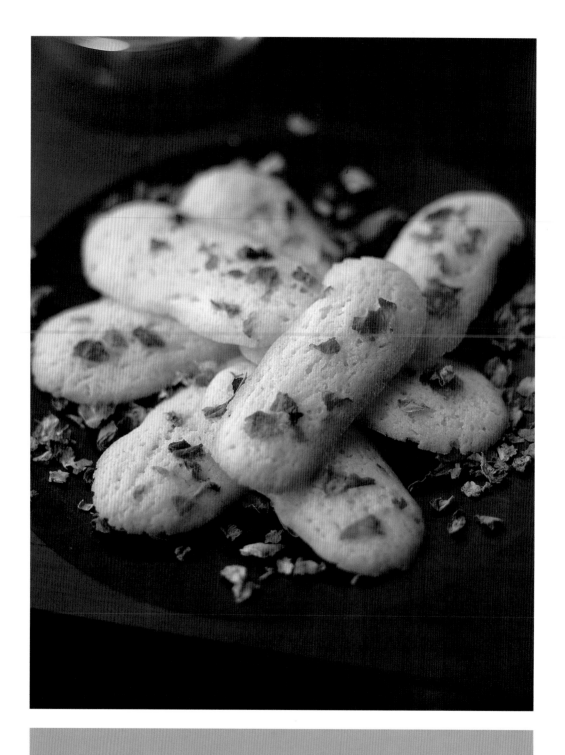

Langues de chat

Langues de chat

Delicate

Langues de chat means "cats' tongues" in French, and these are very appropriately named. Thin, tongue-shaped biscuits that can be pepped up with a few additional flavourings if liked.

Makes approx. 36–48

125g (4½oz) **butter, softened**
125g (4½oz) **caster sugar**
3 **egg whites**
125g (4½oz) **plain flour**

Optional extras (choose only one from the following):
2 tsp **lavender flowers / dried rose petals / fennel seeds or crystallized fruits,** finely chopped
½ tsp **ground cinnamon**
½ tsp **vanilla extract**
Grated rind of 1 **orange or lemon**

Preheat the oven to 200°C/400°F/ Gas mark 6. Line a baking sheet with baking parchment.

Beat the butter and sugar together until pale and creamy. In a separate bowl whisk the egg whites until stiff, then gradually fold them into the butter mixture. Sift in the flour and gently fold into the mixture.

Fit a piping bag with a medium-sized plain nozzle and spoon in the mixture. Pipe the mixture into 7.5-cm (3-in) long fingers, no thicker than 1cm (½in) wide, leaving a little space between them to allow for spreading.

Sprinkle with the optional extras of our choice if liked and bake for 5–8 minutes, or until crispy and pale golden around the edges. Allow to cool completely.

Mini macaroons

Coconutty

Macaroons are simplicity at its best. Only four ingredients are required, yet they produce an impressive result.

Makes 24–36

175g (6oz) **sweetened desiccated coconut**
150g (5½oz) **caster sugar**
2 **egg whites,** lightly beaten
4 sheets **edible rice paper**

Preheat the oven to 170°C/325°F/ Gas mark 3.

In a large bowl combine the coconut and caster sugar. Add the egg whites and stir in to form a fairly firm mixture.

Lay out the rice paper on one or two baking sheets. Shape the mixture into heaped teaspoon-sized balls and place on the rice paper, pressing down gently to flatten.

Bake for 10–12 minutes, or until lightly golden. Remove from the oven and allow to cool on the baking sheets. Tear away any excess rice paper to serve.

■ *Try adding some grated lime rind or finely shredded kaffir lime leaves to the mixture for a more exotic macaroon.*

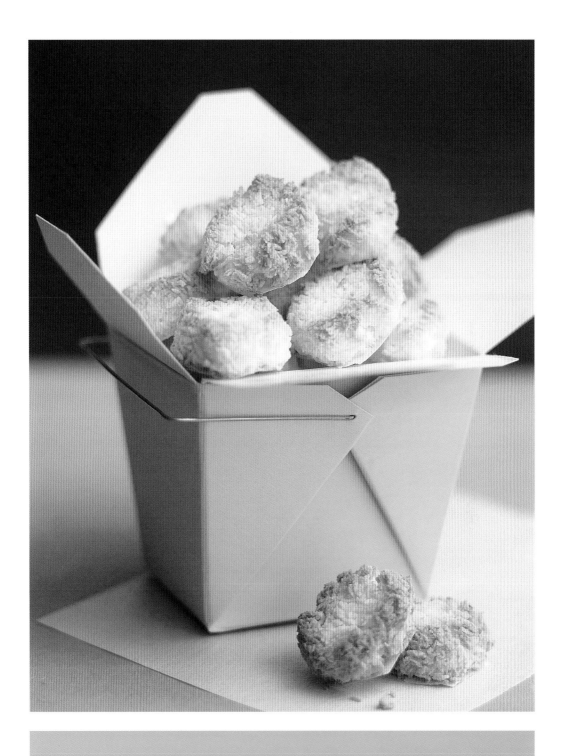

Mini macaroons

Spiced cigar cookies

Impressive

These biscuits are very delicate and require quick hands. You must work fast to achieve a neat-looking cylindrical shape but they are well worth the effort and patience!

Makes 24–30

2 **egg whites**
90g (3¼oz) **caster sugar**
50g (1¾oz) **plain flour**
½–1 tsp **ground cinnamon, mixed spice or ginger (or any other spice of choice)**
4 Tbsp **butter,** melted

Beat the egg whites in a large clean bowl until soft peaks form. Gradually beat in the sugar until the mixture becomes thick and glossy. In a separate bowl combine the flour and spice. Add the flour mixture and the melted butter to the egg white mixture and mix until just combined. Allow the mixture to rest for about 15 minutes.

Preheat the oven to 180°C/350°F/ Gas mark 4. Line a baking sheet with baking parchment.

Spoon teaspoonfuls of the mixture on to the baking parchment and, using the back of a spoon, spread evenly and thinly to about 8cm (3¼in) in diameter. Make sure the mixture is evenly spread to ease the next stage. Only bake three or four per tray. Bake for 3 minutes, or until lightly golden.

Remove from the oven and wait for 30 seconds before loosening the biscuits using a flat palette knife. Return to the oven for a further 15–20 seconds to soften the biscuits again.

Remove from the oven and, working quickly, turn the cookies over and roll up thinly around a lightly greased wooden spoon handle to obtain a cylinder shape. Slide off and set aside. Repeat until all the mixture is used up.

Almond and vanilla triangles

Crisp

These are a great accompaniment to ice cream. Shaped like a triangle, they act as a perfect scoop.

Makes 16–20

1 Tbsp **plain flour,** sifted
1 Tbsp **ground almonds**
45g (1½oz) **caster sugar**
1 **egg white,** lightly beaten
½ tsp **vanilla extract**
2 Tbsp **melted butter**
30g (1oz) **flaked almonds**

Preheat the oven to 180°C/350°F/Gas mark 4. Line the base of a 30 x 25-cm (12 x 10-in) baking tray with baking parchment.

Combine the flour, almonds and sugar in a small bowl. Stir in the egg white, vanilla extract and melted butter and mix to a smooth batter. Pour the mixture into the prepared tray and spread evenly over the surface. Sprinkle over the flaked almonds.

Bake for 12–14 minutes, or until firm when gently pressed and lightly golden in colour. Remove from the oven and transfer the baking parchment to a chopping board.

Trim the edges, working as quickly as possible, then cut the rectangle in half lengthways. Cut each half into about 8–10 triangles and transfer to a wire rack. Allow to cool completely before serving.

Sugar butter biscuits

Colourful

These dessert-time biscuits will really appeal to the kids if you cut them into different shapes and top each with different coloured sugars.

Makes approx. 24–30

275g (9¾oz) **plain flour**
200g (7oz) **firm butter**
100g (3½oz) **icing sugar**
2 **egg yolks**
1 quantity **Clear sugar glaze**
  (see page 170)
Coloured sugars (see page 167)

Put the flour and butter in a food processor and process until the mixture resembles fine breadcrumbs. Add the sugar and egg yolks and process until the mixture starts to form a dough. Alternatively, cut the butter into small cubes and add to the flour. Using your fingers, rub the butter into the flour until it makes fine breadcrumbs. Add the sugar and egg yolks and mix to a smooth dough. On a lightly floured surface knead the

dough until it comes together. Shape into a ball and wrap in baking parchment then chill for at least 30 minutes.

Preheat the oven to 190°C/375°F/ Gas mark 5. Line a baking sheet with baking parchment. Roll out the dough on a lightly floured surface to about 5mm (¼in) thick and cut into your chosen shapes. Bake for 8–10 minutes, or until lightly golden in colour. Remove from the oven and allow to cool for a few minutes on the baking sheet then transfer to a wire rack to and allow to cool completely.

While the cookies are still warm brush them with the sugar glaze then sprinkle over the coloured sugar of your choice. Leave to cool completely so the sugar glaze sets.

Chocolate peanut tuiles

Chocolate lace

Tuiles, meaning "tile" in French, are named after the tiled roofs of Provence. Here tuiles are made up of two classic ingredients to make one, lacy delight. Serve them plain, or with vanilla ice cream and a drizzle of chocolate sauce.

Makes 44–48

5 Tbsp **salted butter**
100g (3½oz) **caster sugar**
3 Tbsp **golden syrup**
1 Tbsp **double cream**
35g (1¼oz) **plain flour**
40g (1½oz) **cocoa powder**
¼ tsp **salt**
100g (3½oz) **salted peanuts,** chopped

Preheat the oven to 180°C/350°F/ Gas mark 4. Line baking sheets with baking parchment. For rounded tuiles, have a rolling pin at hand.

Combine the butter, sugar, golden syrup and cream in a heavy saucepan and bring to the boil over medium heat, stirring constantly. Add the flour, cocoa powder and salt, and continue stirring until the batter is thick. Stir in the peanuts.

Drop level teaspoonfuls of the batter (level off each teaspoon with a knife) on to the baking sheet, approximately six mounds to a sheet (see tip). Bake until flat, lacy and bubbling, about 5–7 minutes. Allow to cool for 2 minutes, then quickly flip the tuiles over.

Leave to cool if you want flat tuiles. For rounded tuiles, quickly place 2–3 tuiles around a rolling pin to shape then slide them on to a wire rack and allow to cool. If the tuiles become too stiff to shape, return them briefly to the oven. Continue with the remaining batter.

Store the tuiles in an airtight container for up to 1 week.

■ *Cook the tuiles six at a time. Any more, and working quickly becomes too difficult.*

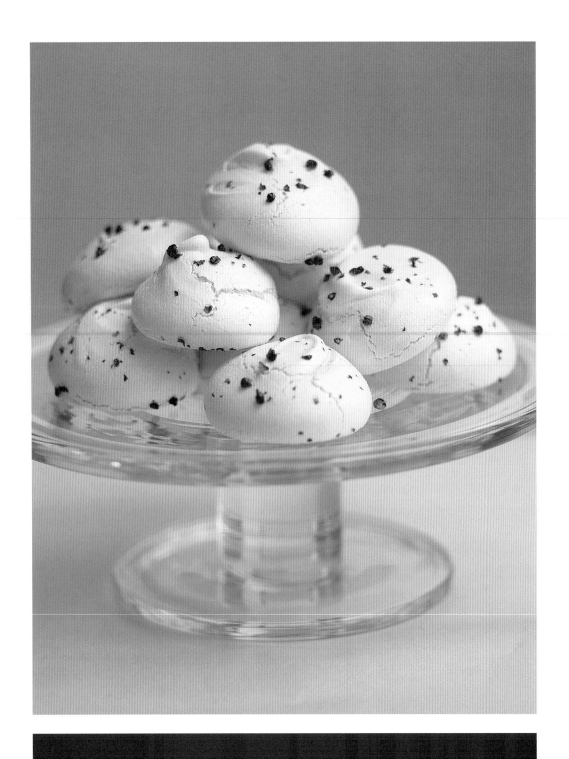

Pink peppercorn meringues

Pink peppercorn meringues

Lush

Piquancy meets sweet innocence in these little cloud-like meringues. The combination may seem odd, but the hint of heat is a surprisingly welcome contrast to the delicate sweetness of meringues.

Makes 60–70

6 **egg whites**
⅛ tsp **cream of tartar**
420g (15oz) **caster sugar**
1 Tbsp **balsamic vinegar**
1½ tsp **pink peppercorns,** coarsely ground
Icing sugar, for dusting (optional)

Preheat the oven to 140°C/275°F/Gas mark 1. Line a baking sheet with baking parchment.

Place the egg whites into the bowl of an electric mixer. The bowl should be very clean. Beat the egg whites until foamy. Add the cream of tartar and continue to beat until soft peaks form. Beat the sugar in gradually, one spoonful at a time, until the whites are glossy. This will take about 10 minutes. (It may seem daunting, but stick with it!) Gently stir in the vinegar and half the peppercorns.

Spoon mounded tablespoonfuls of the meringue mixture on to the baking sheet. Sprinkle with the remaining peppercorns. Bake for 40–45 minutes, until the whites are set and are just beginning to turn golden. Remove from the oven and allow to cool. If not serving immediately, store the meringues in an airtight container for up to 1 week.

Persian lace cookies

Rose-scented

These crisp, lacy cookies, studded with vibrant pistachio nuts and a touch of rosewater, are bursting with Persian flavours.

Makes approx. 48

140g (5oz) **plain flour**
¼ tsp **salt**
150g (5½oz) **light brown sugar**
125ml (4fl oz) **golden syrup**
120g (4½oz) **butter**
100g (3½oz) **pistachio nuts,** chopped
1 Tbsp **rosewater**

Preheat the oven to 190°C/375°F/ Gas mark 5. Lightly grease or line two baking sheets with parchment paper.

Sift the flour with the salt in a bowl and set aside. Combine the brown sugar, golden syrup and butter in a saucepan over medium heat. Bring to the boil, stirring occasionally. Boil for 30 seconds. Remove from the heat and stir into the flour mixture together with the chopped pistachio nuts and rosewater.

Drop the batter in rounded teaspoonfuls, 5cm (2in) apart, on to the baking sheets. Bake for 7–10 minutes, until the edges are lightly browned. Allow to cool on the baking sheets.

Carefully remove cookies from the baking sheets and store in an airtight container for up to 5 days.

Persian lace cookies

Crystallized ginger lace cookies

Spiced

Slivers of almonds and sweet ginger flow through these crisp, lacy cookies.

Makes approx. 48

140g (5oz) **plain flour**
¼ tsp **salt**
1 tsp **ground ginger**
150g (5½oz) **light brown sugar**
125ml (4fl oz) **golden syrup**
8 Tbsp **butter**
110g (4oz) **almonds,** chopped
½ Tbsp **crystallized ginger,** finely chopped

Preheat the oven to 180°C/350°F/ Gas mark 4. Lightly grease or line two baking sheets with baking parchment.

Sift the flour together with the salt and ground ginger in a bowl. Set aside.

Combine the brown sugar, golden syrup and butter in a saucepan over medium heat. Bring to the boil, stirring occasionally. Remove from the heat and add the chopped almonds and crystallized ginger. Stir into the flour mixture.

Drop the batter by the rounded ½ teaspoonful, 5cm (2in) apart, on to the baking sheets. Bake for 9–10 minutes, until the edges are lightly browned. Allow to cool on the baking sheets.

Carefully remove cookies from baking sheets and store in an airtight container for up to 5 days.

Five-spice sponge fingers

Classic

Génoise, a whole egg sponge cake, is the basis for sponge fingers. The addition of a little more flour and the Chinese five-spice mixture gives these fingers shape and a unique flavour. For classic sponge fingers, omit the five-spice powder and substitute vanilla for the orange extract.

Makes approx. 72

3 Tbsp **butter,** melted
175g (6oz) **plain flour,** sifted
⅛ tsp **salt**
½ tsp **Chinese five-spice powder**
2 **eggs**
4 **egg yolks**
70g (2½oz) **caster sugar**
1 tsp **orange extract**
Icing sugar, for dusting

Preheat the oven to 200°C/400°F/ Gas mark 6. Line two baking sheets with baking parchment. Have a piping bag fitted with a 1.5-cm (⅝-in) plain nozzle ready and waiting.

Pour the melted butter into a large mixing bowl. Set aside. Combine the flour, salt and five-spice powder together and set aside.

Combine the eggs, yolks and 1 Tbsp sugar in the bowl of an electric mixer and use the whisk attachment to combine. Add the remaining sugar and whisk by hand until smooth. Re-attach the whisk attachment and whip the mixture on medium speed until soft, pale and tripled in volume, about 4–5 minutes. Whisk in the orange extract and beat for a few seconds longer. Lift the whisk from the batter – a ribbon trail should form on the surface and should hold its place for 10 seconds. If it sinks to the bottom, continue beating.

Sprinkle the egg mixture with one third of the flour mixture. Using a rubber spatula, gently fold together just until the flour disappears. Continue adding the flour by one thirds until just combined. Be gentle.

Slowly add this batter, a spoonful at a time, into the bowl with the melted butter. Fold together as you go with a rubber spatula. Scoop the batter into the piping bag and pipe sponge fingers 1.5cm (⅝in) wide, 8cm (3¼in) long and 1.5cm (⅝in) apart. Using a sieve, dust the sponge fingers generously with icing sugar. Bake for 5–6 minutes, until firm but spongy, and not yet golden. Carefully transfer the sponge fingers, with the baking parchment still attached, to a wire rack and allow to cool completely. Separate any attached fingers gently with a knife.

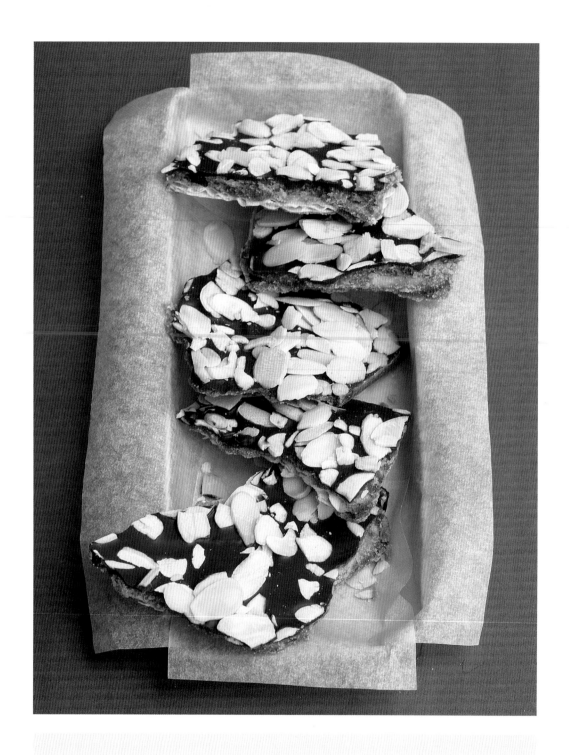

Bark

Bark

Addictive

Aunt Jude is to thank for this Wilson family gathering staple. She calls it "barque", which adds quite a sophisticated edge to this delicacy. And people will think it is a delicacy – you don't have to tell them what the secret ingredient is!

Makes approx. 42 pieces

220g (7¾oz) **butter**
120g (4½oz) **brown sugar**
180g (6oz) **cream crackers**
200g (7oz) **plain chocolate chips or plain chocolate,** roughly chopped
100g (3½oz) **sliced almonds,** lightly toasted

Preheat the oven to 200°C/400°F/ Gas mark 6.

Line a baking tray with foil, shiny-side up. Cover the foil with the crackers. Do not overlap.

Melt the butter and sugar in a saucepan over medium heat. Bring the mixture to the boil, stirring well to ensure the butter and sugar are well blended. Pour the mixture over the crackers and bake for 2–4 minutes, until the butter mixture begins to bubble. Watch carefully. Remove from the oven and sprinkle with chocolate. Bake for a further 1 minute, until the chocolate is soft. Remove from the oven and spread the chocolate evenly to form an icing layer. Sprinkle with almonds. Place the tray in the fridge for about 1 hour, until cool. Remove the bark from the foil and break roughly into 5-cm square pieces.

Store the bark in an airtight container for up to 5 days, or freeze for up to 2 months.

Celebration cookies

Food has a powerful way of triggering our senses and transporting us to past events and celebrations. Cookies, despite their diminutive size, are especially effective transporters. Celebration cookies encourage creativity. Dainty touches are expected. Festive flavours are called for, and special ingredients are sourced. Batters are stirred, shaped and baked. And suddenly, with a simple waft through the kitchen, we are taken back to last year's celebration.

Bakers around the world have a collection of celebration cookies. They are passed down through the generations, connecting us through our senses to events of the past. The ritual of baking celebration cookies acts to enforce not only the significance of the recipe, but also the event itself. Anzac biscuits (page 144) remind Australians and New Zealanders of their militaristic past. Orange and rum shortbread (page 154) transports many straight to Christmas. Rugelach (page 163) signifies a Jewish celebration. Valentine stained glass cookies (page 159) remind us of loved ones on Valentine's Day. And, as we bake these recipes, we are creating future memories for those around us.

Who could have guessed that baking a cookie could hold such significance?

Polenta Christmas biscuits with orange icing

Fragrant

Polenta gives these biscuits a slightly crunchy texture. Attach ribbons to each cookie and decorate the tree with an assortment of Christmas shapes.

Makes approx. 40

250g (9oz) **butter,** softened
125g (4½oz) **icing sugar**
1 **egg yolk**
Grated **rind of** 1 **orange**
300g (10½oz) **plain flour**
75g (2¾oz) **polenta or fine cornmeal**
2 Tbsp **cornflour**
1 tsp **cardamom seeds,** crushed

To decorate:
1 quantity **Orange icing (see variation
   to Lemon icing, page 165)**
Silver balls
**Ribbon or string (if making
   Christmas tree decorations)**

Beat the butter and sugar in a large bowl until pale and creamy. Add the egg yolk and orange rind and beat until just combined. In a separate bowl combine the remaining ingredients and stir into the butter mixture. Stir the mixture until it all comes together and forms a ball. Wrap the ball in baking parchment and chill for 20–30 minutes.

Preheat the oven to 190°C/375°F/ Gas mark 5. Roll the mixture out on a floured surface to about 7mm (⅜in) thick.

Using a cutter of your choice, cut out as many shapes as possible from the rolled mixture and place on a baking sheet lined with baking parchment. Re-shape the remaining dough and roll again until all the mixture is used up. If you want to use the biscuits as Christmas tree decorations, make a small hole with a skewer for the ribbon or string at the top of the shape.

Bake for 10–12 minutes, or until golden and firm. Allow to cool on a wire rack. When the biscuits have cooled completely prepare the icing. Spread the icing over the biscuits, allow to set then decorate as liked with silver balls.

Polenta Christmas biscuits with orange icing

Spiced easter cookies

Spiced Easter cookies

Crisp

These biscuits make a welcome change from chocolate Easter eggs. Decorate them with coloured icings and they will appeal to both young and old.

Makes 36–48, depending on shapes chosen

100g (3½oz) **butter,** softened
200g (7oz) **caster sugar**
1 **egg,** beaten
300g (10½oz) **plain flour**
1 tsp **baking powder**
2 tsp **ground mixed spice or ground cinnamon**

To decorate:
1 quantity **Coloured icing (see page 164)**

In a large bowl beat the butter and caster sugar together until pale and creamy. Add the egg and beat until the mixture is light and fluffy. In a separate bowl combine the flour, baking powder and mixed spice. Add to the butter mixture and mix thoroughly. Add 1 tsp cold water to bring the dough together if you need to. Wrap the mixture in baking parchment and chill for at least 30 minutes.

Preheat the oven to 180°C/350°F/ Gas mark 4. Line two baking sheets with baking parchment.

On a lightly floured surface, roll out the dough to about 4mm (¼in) thick and, using cookie cutters, stamp out shapes. Using a palette knife, lift the shapes carefully on to the baking parchment.

Bake for 15–18 minutes, or until lightly golden in colour. Allow to cool on a wire rack then ice, as liked.

Anzac biscuits

Nourishing

Anzac biscuits touch the hearts of all New Zealanders and Australians. Based on an old recipe for Scottish oatcakes, they were made by soldiers' wives and children and sent to the men during the First World War in order to keep them well nourished. They were so good that even today they are top of the hit list!

Makes 20

150g (5½oz) **plain flour**
100g (3½oz) **sweetened desiccated coconut**
100g (3½oz) **light brown sugar**
100g (3½oz) **porridge oats**
125g (4½oz) **butter**
1 Tbsp **golden syrup**
½ tsp **bicarbonate of soda**
2 Tbsp **boiling water**

Preheat the oven to 160°C/325°F/Gas mark 3. Line a large baking sheet with baking parchment.

Place the flour, coconut, sugar and oats in a large bowl and mix well. Place the butter and golden syrup in a saucepan over medium heat and melt. Put the bicarbonate of soda in a small bowl and pour over the boiling water, stirring to combine. Add the bicarbonate of soda mixture to the saucepan and stir. Pour this mixture over the dry mixture and stir all the ingredients together.

Roll teaspoonfuls of the mixture into balls and place on the lined baking sheet, leaving a little space between them to allow for spreading. Flatten each ball gently with a fork.

Bake for 15–20 minutes, or until golden brown. Allow to cool slightly on the baking sheet before transferring to a wire rack.

Anzac biscuits

Fortune cookies

Impressive

This is a fun way to liven up a dinner party. Be imaginative with your fortunes and you'll be guaranteed some laughs. Make them a few days in advance and store them in an airtight container.

Makes 18

2 **egg whites**
90g (3¼oz) **caster sugar**
50g (1¾oz) **plain flour**
4 Tbsp **butter,** melted

Beat the egg whites in a large clean bowl until soft peaks form. Gradually beat in the sugar until the mixture becomes thick and glossy. Add the flour and melted butter to the egg white mixture and mix until just combined. Allow the mixture to rest for about 15 minutes while you prepare your fortunes.

Preheat the oven to 180°C/350°F/ Gas mark 4. Line a baking sheet with baking parchment.

Cut a piece of plain white paper into small strips about 5mm (¼in) wide and 4cm (1½in) long. Be imaginative and write some fortunes.

Spoon teaspoonfuls of the mixture on to the baking parchment and, using the back of a spoon, spread evenly and thinly to a circle about 8cm (3¼in) in diameter. Make sure the mixture is evenly spread to ease the next stage. You will need to work in batches: only bake three to four cookies per baking sheet. Bake for 3 minutes, or until lightly golden.

Remove from the oven and wait for 30 seconds before loosening the biscuits using a flat palette knife. Return to the oven for a further 15–20 seconds to soften the biscuits again. Remove from the oven and, working quickly, turn the cookies over and place a fortune in the centre. Fold in half and half again. Sit inside a small shot glass or bowl until cool and crisp. Repeat until all the mixture is used up.

Middle eastern walnut and honey crisps

Spiced

This is based on a recipe of my Grandmother's. Use the freshest walnuts you can find and the most flavoursome, fragrant honey.

Makes 18–24

125g (4½oz) **butter, softened**
100g (3½oz) **caster sugar**
2 Tbsp **honey**
150g (5½oz) **plain flour**
½ tsp **baking powder**
½ tsp **ground cinnamon**
½ tsp **ground ginger**
100g (3½oz) **freshly shelled walnuts, roughly chopped**

Preheat the oven to 180°C/350°F/ Gas mark 4. Line one or two baking sheets with baking parchment.

Cream the butter and sugar in a large bowl until pale and creamy. Add the honey and beat for a further minute. In a separate bowl, combine the flour, baking powder, cinnamon and ginger. Stir into the butter mixture followed by the chopped walnuts. Mix until everything is just combined. Shape the mixture into tablespoon-sized balls and place on the prepared baking sheets. Press gently with a fork and bake for 12–15 minutes, or until golden.

Kourabiedes

Kourabiedes

Crumbly

These rich, short cookies are traditional Greek Christmas cookies and are perfect served with a nip of brandy.

Makes 20

125g (4½oz) **butter,** softened
50g (1¾oz) **icing sugar,** plus extra for dusting
1 **egg yolk**
1 tsp **vanilla extract**
1 tsp **orange flower water**
150g (5½oz) **plain flour**
1 tsp **baking powder**
150g (5½oz) **ground almonds**

Preheat the oven to 160°C/325°F/ Gas mark 3. Line two baking sheets with baking parchment.

Beat the butter until pale and creamy. Add the icing sugar, egg yolk, vanilla extract and orange flower water and beat until fluffy. Combine the flour, baking powder and ground almonds in a separate bowl then stir into the butter mixture. Using heaped tablespoonfuls of the dough, shape it into sausage shapes about 8cm (3¼in) long then curve into a crescent shape on the baking sheet.

Bake for 15–18 minutes, or until light golden in colour. Allow to cool for about 5 minutes on the baking sheet before dusting with extra icing sugar. Transfer to a wire rack and allow to cool completely.

Double ginger crackle cookies

Sweet ginger

This recipe comes from Grammy Brownlee, who makes these chewy cookies, studded with pieces of crystallized ginger, at Christmas time. It's cookies like these that make you wish Christmas came more than once a year…

Makes 36

160g (5½oz) **butter**
200g (7oz) **caster sugar, plus** 100g
  (3½oz) **extra,** for rolling
1 **egg**
75ml (2½fl oz) **molasses or treacle**
300g (10½oz) **plain flour**
2 tsp **bicarbonate of soda**
¼ tsp **salt**
1 Tbsp **ground ginger**
1 tsp **ground cinnamon**
1 tsp **ground cloves**
100g (3½oz) **crystallized ginger,**
  finely chopped

Preheat the oven to 180°C/350°F/ Gas mark 4.

In a large mixing bowl cream the butter and 200g (7oz) sugar until smooth. Beat in the egg and molasses. In a separate bowl, sift together the flour, bicarbonate of soda, salt, ginger, cinnamon and cloves. Add to the butter mixture along with the crystallized ginger and stir just until combined.

Put the remaining sugar in a shallow bowl. Shape the dough into rounded tablespoon-sized balls (roughly 3.5cm/1½in wide) and roll the balls in sugar. Place the balls 5cm (2in) apart on ungreased or parchment-lined baking sheets.

Bake for 8–10 minutes, until the edges are cracked and the centres just set. Allow to cool on baking sheets for 5 minutes before transferring to wire racks to cool completely.

Portuguese star anise cookies

Liquorice

I first stumbled upon these Portuguese cookies flavoured with star anise while flipping through a Portuguese cookbook at the library. They are a traditional cookie, not necessarily festive in Portugal, but my version of the recipe has become part of our tea-time Christmas ritual. The addition of yeast, orange rind and a splash of port make for a very intriguing combination of flavours.

Makes 50–55

400g (14oz) **plus** 1 tsp **caster sugar**
125ml (4fl oz) **lukewarm water**
1 Tbsp **fast-acting dried yeast**
650g (1lb 7oz) **plain flour**
½ tsp **bicarbonate of soda**
½ tsp **salt**
1 Tbsp **ground star anise**
1 tsp **ground cinnamon**
1 Tbsp **orange rind**, grated
2 **eggs**
1 tsp **vanilla extract**
2 Tbsp **vegetable oil**
1 Tbsp **port**
120g (4½oz) **butter,** melted and
    cooled

Preheat the oven to 180°C/350°F/
Gas mark 4.

Dissolve 1 tsp sugar in lukewarm water. Sprinkle over the yeast and leave to stand for 10 minutes. Foam should appear over the surface.

Meanwhile, sift together the flour, bicarbonate of soda, salt, ground star anise and cinnamon. Stir in the orange rind. Set aside.

In a separate bowl, whisk together the eggs, vanilla extract, vegetable oil, port and butter. Whisk the yeast mixture, and combine with the egg mixture. Gradually add to the flour mixture, stirring until the dough is combined.

Flour a work surface and knead the dough for 8–10 minutes. The dough will be quite stiff. Form into a ball and place in a lightly greased bowl. Cover with a tea towel and leave to rise for 1 hour. The dough will rise very little – don't panic!

Form the dough into rounded tablespoon-sized balls and place, 5cm (2in) apart, on greased or parchment-lined baking sheets.

Bake for 15 minutes, until golden. Allow to cool on the baking sheet then transfer to a wire rack and allow to cool completely.

Lavender sugar cookies

Dainty

Lavender buds lend a dainty quality to these traditional cookies. The flavour is created by blitzing the buds with sugar and leaving them to infuse overnight. Lavender can, however, be omitted if a plain sugar cookie is required. Experiment with different shapes, sizes and decorations, depending on the celebration.

Makes approx. 48

250g (9oz) **caster sugar**
2 Tbsp **lavender buds**
220g (7¾oz) **butter,** softened
1 tsp **vanilla extract**
300g (10½oz) **plain flour**
½ tsp **salt**
½ tsp **bicarbonate of soda**

Place all the sugar and lavender buds in a food processor and blitz to break up the buds. Transfer the sugar to a covered container and allow to infuse, preferably overnight.

Pass the sugar through a sieve to remove the larger bud bits. Combine 220g (7¾oz) sugar, butter and vanilla in a mixing bowl and, using an electric mixer, beat until smooth. In a separate bowl, sift together the flour, salt and bicarbonate of soda. Using a wooden spoon, slowly stir the flour into the butter mixture until smooth. Divide the dough into two balls, cover with clingfilm and chill for 1 hour.

Preheat the oven to 190°C/375°F/ Gas mark 5. Lightly grease or line two baking trays with baking parchment.

Lightly flour a work surface and roll the balls, one at a time, to 3mm (⅛in) thick. Cut into shapes and sprinkle with the reserved sugar. Transfer to baking sheets. Bake for 8–12 minutes, until very lightly golden. The exact timing will depend on the size of the shapes.

Allow to cool on the baking sheets for a few minutes then transfer to wire racks and allow to cool completely.

Lavender sugar cookies

Orange and rum shortbread

Decadent

This recipe is a variation on our Classic shortbread featured in the Coffee-time chapter (see page 115). Light, buttery shortbread coupled with a splash of rum and candied orange peel is as festive as it gets. The crown of creamy icing is just the icing on the, well, shortbread.

Makes 40 x 5-cm (2-in) diameter cookies

50g (1¾oz) **icing sugar**, sifted
450g (1lb) **butter**, softened
1½ Tbsp **dark rum**
525g (1lb 3oz) **plain flour**, sifted
60g (2¼oz) **cornflour**, sifted
200g (7oz) **shop-bought candied orange peel**, finely chopped

Preheat the oven to 180°C/350°F/Gas mark 4. Line two baking sheets with baking parchment.

Combine the icing sugar and butter in a large mixing bowl and beat until very light and fluffy. Beat in the rum. In a separate bowl combine the flour and cornflour. Using a wooden spoon, stir the flour mixture into the butter mixture and work together until combined. Stir in the candied orange peel.

Gather the dough and divide into two equal mounds. Flour a work surface and roll the first mound into a 24-cm (9½-in) wide circle, almost 1.5cm (⅝in) thick. Cut the dough into the desired shapes and place on parchment-lined baking sheets. (We used a 5-cm (2-in) wide round cookie cutter.)

Bake for 20–22 minutes, until slightly golden. Allow to cool for 5 minutes then transfer to wire racks and allow to cool completely. Meanwhile, continue baking the remaining shortbread.

Top, if desired, with Vanilla butter icing (see page 166) and our Candied peel (see page 168)

Fruitcake cookies

Moist

I must admit that fruitcake was never my idea of festive bliss. Until, that is, I tasted it in cookie form!

Makes 40

50g (1¾oz) **whole hazelnuts**
110g (4oz) **butter**
70g (2½oz) **dark brown sugar**
1 **egg**
145g (5½oz) **plain flour**
½ tsp **bicarbonate of soda**
⅛ tsp **salt**
375g (13oz) **dates,** finely chopped
175g (6oz) **candied peel**
50g (1¾oz) **walnut pieces**
50g (1¾oz) **pecan nuts,** chopped

Preheat the oven to 180°C/350°F/ Gas mark 4.

Toast the whole hazelnuts in a dry frying pan on the hob until fragrant and slightly golden. Tip into a clean tea towel and rub the nuts together to loosen and remove the skins. Skins are stubborn so don't worry if bits remain.

Cream the butter and brown sugar in an electric mixer until light and fluffy. Add the egg and beat until smooth. Sift the flour with the bicarbonate of soda and salt. Stir into the butter mixture just until combined. In a separate bowl, mix the dates, candied peel and nuts. Stir into the batter. The dough will be heavy on fruit and nuts, light on batter.

Roll the dough into teaspoon-sized balls and place on lightly greased or parchment-lined baking sheets. Bake for 12 minutes until golden, but slightly soft in the centre. Allow to cool on the baking sheets for 5 minutes then transfer to wire racks and allow to cool completely.

Store in an airtight container for up to 5 days, or freeze for up to 2 months.

Coconut date balls

Rich

These wonderfully sweet, coconut-covered balls are an essential addition to any festive sweet tray. The recipe has been handed down through the family from my great-grandmother Brownlee. I wonder if she used Rice Krispies® way back then?

Makes approx. 24

220g (7¾oz) **caster sugar**
2 **eggs,** lightly beaten
150g (5½oz) **dates,** finely chopped
1 tsp **vanilla extract**
80g (3oz) **Rice Krispies®**
50g (1¾oz) **walnuts,** chopped
100g (3½oz) **sweetened desiccated coconut**

Line two baking sheets with greaseproof paper or baking parchment.

Combine the sugar, beaten eggs and chopped dates in a large saucepan. Place the pan over medium heat and cook the mixture, stirring occasionally, for 7 minutes. Remove from the heat and add the vanilla extract, Rice Krispies® and walnuts. Stir well. Allow to cool for 10–15 minutes.

Place the coconut in a shallow bowl. Wet your hands with cold water and roll the date mixture into small, teaspoon-sized balls. The mixture will be sticky, so keep cold water on hand. Roll the balls in coconut and place on the baking sheets. Allow balls to firm up at room temperature.

Store in airtight containers for up to 5 days, the layers separated by greaseproof paper, or freeze for up to 2 months.

Chocolate peanut butter balls

Dangerous

Christmas wouldn't be Christmas without feasting on these decadent balls on Christmas Eve at my grandmother's house. They were also the most popular dessert at my wedding. The recipe can be doubled, tripled or even quadrupled, and freezes well.

Makes approx. 40 rounded tablespoon-sized balls or 60–70 rounded teaspoon-sized balls

250g (9oz) **smooth peanut butter**
4 Tbsp **butter,** softened
125g (4½oz) **icing sugar**
50g (1¾oz) **walnuts,** chopped and toasted
50g (1¾oz) **sweetened desiccated coconut**
20g (¾oz) **Rice Krispies®**

For the coating:
200g (7oz) **chocolate chips or plain chocolate,** roughly chopped
1 Tbsp **butter**

Line two baking sheets with greaseproof paper or baking parchment.

Combine the peanut butter, butter and icing sugar in a large mixing bowl and stir well until smooth. Add the walnuts, coconut and Rice Krispies® and stir until combined. Cover and chill for 1 hour.

To make the coating, combine the chocolate and butter in a heatproof bowl over a saucepan of simmering water. Stir until melted and remove from the heat.

Form the peanut butter mixture into tablespoon-sized balls and, using two spoons, dip the balls into chocolate. Place on the baking sheets. If the chocolate gets thick, place the bowl over simmering water and re-heat.

Store the balls layered between greaseproof paper in airtight containers in the fridge for up to 1 week. Alternatively, freeze for up to 2 months.

Valentine stained glass cookies

Valentine stained glass cookies

Eye-catching

These little gems are almost too pretty to eat!

Makes approx. 40

110g (4oz) **butter,** softened
110g (4oz) **caster sugar**
125ml (4fl oz) **honey**
1 **egg**
1 tsp **vanilla extract**
450g (1lb) **plain flour**
1 tsp **baking powder**
½ tsp **bicarbonate of soda**
½ tsp **salt**
5 tubes **hard boiled sweets**

Cream the butter, sugar, honey, egg and vanilla extract until smooth. In a separate bowl, sift the flour, baking powder, bicarbonate of soda and salt. Add to the butter mixture and stir to combine. Gather the dough into a ball in the bowl and chill for 2 hours.

Preheat the oven to 180°C/350°F/ Gas mark 4. Line two baking sheets with foil, shiny-side up.

Lightly flour a work surface and roll out the dough 1cm (½in) thick. Using lightly floured 6–8-cm (2½ –3¼-in) heart-shaped cutters, cut out heart shapes. Cut a smaller heart shape within the cookie, leaving a 1.5–2-cm (⅝–¾-in) border of dough. (This is easily done by making a cardboard heart-shaped cut-out and tracing around it with a knife.) Remove the centre of each heart and set aside. Place the cut-outs on the baking sheets.

Crush the sweets between two sheets of greaseproof paper or baking parchment using a rolling pin or mallet. Spoon into the centre of the hearts. Bake for 6–8 minutes, until the sweets have melted and the cookies are golden. Allow the cookies to cool completely before removing them carefully from the foil using a spatula.

Meanwhile, gather up any dough scraps and re-roll to make more cookies. Only re-roll the dough once; any more and it will become too tough.

Easter lemon curd sandwiches

Delicate

Easter-time treats, for me, aren't just about chocolate. They can also mean fresh flavours and pretty delicacies that signify spring. Here it is, in cookie form!

Makes 18–24

1 quantity Langues de chat,
  baked and cooled (see page 123)

For the lemon curd:
100g (3½oz) unsalted butter
150g (5½oz) caster sugar
Juice and grated rind of 3 lemons
3 eggs, beaten

Make the lemon curd: put the butter, sugar, lemon juice and rind in a heatproof bowl. Place over a saucepan of simmering water and stir over low heat until the sugar has dissolved and the mixture is warm. Whisk the warm lemon mixture into the beaten eggs and strain through a non-metallic sieve. Return the mixture to the heatproof bowl and place over the still simmering water. Stir occasionally until the mixture thickens and coats the back of a wooden spoon. Do not allow the mixture to boil or it will curdle.

Spoon the lemon curd into a bowl and allow to cool. If making the curd in advance, pour the mixture into hot, sterilized jars and seal well. The lemon curd will keep for up to 1 month, stored in a cool place.

Line two baking sheets with greaseproof paper. Place half of the langues de chat underside-up on them. Spoon the lemon curd into a piping bag fitted with a plain nozzle (or a plastic bag with the corner snipped off). Pipe the lemon curd on to the langues de chat, then top with another langues de chat, rounded-side up, to form a sandwich.

The sandwiched cookies will keep, layered between sheets of greaseproof paper or baking parchment in an airtight container in the fridge for 24 hours. Before serving, dust the sandwiches liberally with icing sugar.

Easter lemon curd sandwiches

Rugelach

Rugelach

Warming

Rugelach is a traditional Jewish holiday cookie with jam, nuts, raisins and cinnamon within a soft dough. They are worth the effort, any time of the year.

Makes 48

For the dough:
1 x 225-g (8-oz) tub **cream cheese**
220g (7¾oz) **unsalted butter**
50g (1¾oz) **caster sugar**
1 tsp **vanilla extract**
325g (11½oz) **plain flour**
¼ tsp **salt**

For the filling:
75g (2¾oz) **caster sugar**
50g (1¾oz) **light brown sugar**
½ tsp **ground cinnamon**
100g (3½oz) **raisins**
100g (3½oz) **walnuts**, chopped
110g (4oz) **apricot jam**

For the topping:
75 ml (2½fl oz) **milk**
2 Tbsp **caster sugar**
1 tsp **ground cinnamon**

Line a baking sheet with baking parchment. In a mixing bowl blend the cream cheese and butter until soft. Beat in the sugar and vanilla extract. Slowly add the flour and salt until incorporated. Divide the dough into four portions and cover each with clingfilm. Refrigerate for at least 2 hours.

To make the filling combine the sugars, cinnamon, raisins and walnuts in a bowl and stir until well combined.

Remove the dough from the fridge and allow to stand for 15 minutes until it is soft enough to roll. Preheat the oven to 180°C/350°F/Gas mark 4.

Lightly flour a work surface and roll out each dough portion into a 22-cm (8½-in) circle. Spread the dough evenly with 2 Tbsp of the apricot jam. Sprinkle a quarter of the raisin-walnut filling over the jam and press it down firmly and evenly. Using a sharp knife, cut each dough circle into 12 pieces as if you were cutting a cake. Starting at the wide end, roll up each triangle and bend the ends around to form a slight crescent shape.

Place the Rugelach, point underneath, about 6cm (1½in) apart, on the baking sheet. Refrigerate for at least 30 minutes, or until firm.

Brush the Rugelach with milk, then sprinkle over the sugar and cinnamon. Bake for 18–20 minutes, or until lightly browned. Using a small palette knife, transfer the cookies to wire racks and allow to cool completely. Dust with icing sugar to serve.

Icings and extras

Coloured icings

Yield 175g (6oz)

150g (5½oz) **icing sugar**
2–3 Tbsp **water**
3–4 **drops food colouring of your choice**

Sift the icing sugar into a mixing bowl and stir in the water until the consistency is smooth and shiny but not too runny. Add the your chosen colour and mix until the colour is even.

■ *For a more sophisticated icing, add 2–3 Tbsp liqueur instead of the water.*

Royal icing

Yield – enough to decorate Gingerbread men generously (see page 90)

300g (10½oz) **icing sugar**
2 Tbsp **meringue powder (optional)**
75ml (2½fl oz) **warm water**

Sift the icing sugar with the meringue powder into a mixing bowl and stir in the water until the consistency is smooth and shiny but not too runny. Correct the consistency by adding more icing sugar or water.

■ *Substitute the water with eggnog, if available, for a festive flavour.*

Lemon icing

Yield 175g (6oz)

150g (5½oz) **icing sugar**
2– 3 Tbsp **lemon juice**
Grated rind of 1 **lemon (optional)**

Sift the icing sugar into a mixing bowl and stir in the lemon juice until the consistency is smooth and shiny but not too runny. Spoon the mixture on to the cookies and spread evenly. Top with additional toppings if desired and leave to set.

■ *This can be made using oranges or limes as an alternative*

Chocolate icing

Yield 175g (6oz)

150g (5½oz) **icing sugar**
1½–2 Tbsp **cocoa powder**
1 tsp **butter,** softened
3–4 Tbsp **water**

Sift the icing sugar and cocoa powder into a mixing bowl. Add the softened butter and water, stirring until the consistency is smooth and shiny. Spoon the mixture on to the cookies and spread evenly.

Vanilla butter icing

Yield approx. 225g (8oz)

40g (1½oz) **unsalted butter,** softened
175g (6oz) **icing sugar,** sifted
1–2 drops **vanilla extract**
1–1½ Tbsp **single cream or milk**

Mix the butter vigorously until very soft and creamy. Gradually stir in the sifted icing sugar and vanilla extract. Mix to a smooth paste, adding the cream or milk as needed.

■ *You can colour or flavour this icing as liked by adding a few drops of food colouring or grated citrus rind.*

Chocolate ganache

Ganache is a French term referring to a smooth mixture of chopped chocolate and double cream. Butter can be added to give the ganache a shiny glaze that won't dull. Always choose a chocolate that you like the taste of because this is what will determine the taste and quality of your ganache.

A general guideline:
To make a glaze or coating: 1 part cream to 3 parts chocolate.
To make a rich truffle filling: 1 part cream to 2 parts chocolate.
To make a light filling: 1 part cream to 1 part chocolate.

Yield 175g (6oz)

100g (3½oz) **plain, milk or white chocolate,** chopped
60ml (2fl oz) **double cream**
15g (½oz) **butter**

Place the chocolate in a medium-sized bowl. Set aside. Heat the cream and butter in a small saucepan over medium heat. Bring just to the boil. Immediately pour the boiling cream over the chocolate and allow to stand for 5 minutes. Stir with a whisk until smooth. A teaspoon of liqueur or flavouring can be added at this stage if liked.

Coloured sugars

Yield 50g (1¾oz)

50g (1¾oz) **caster sugar**
3–4 drops **food colouring**

Place caster sugar into a jar with a secure lid. Add food colouring of your choice. Tighten the lid and shake vigorously for a couple of minutes or until the sugar is evenly coloured.

Use coloured sugars to sprinkle over still warm cookies or sprinkle over freshly iced or glazed cookies and leave to set.

Flavoured sugars

Vanilla – put a vanilla pod into a jar of caster sugar and leave to infuse for at least 1 week, shaking occasionally.

Lavender – add about 4–5 heads fresh, unsprayed lavender to a jar of caster sugar and leave to infuse for 3 days.

Spiced – combine about ½ tsp ground mixed spice or cinnamon to 50g (1¾oz) caster sugar and mix to combine. Alternatively, place whole cinnamon sticks or cloves into a jar of caster sugar and leave to infuse for 1–2 weeks.

Citrus – add 1–2 large pieces citrus rind to a jar of caster sugar and leave to infuse for 3–4 days, shaking occasionally.

Dipping chocolate

Dipping cookies in chocolate can be a quick and easy way to add the "wow" factor. Place dipped cookies on a sheet of baking parchment and leave until set.

To melt chocolate in the microwave: place the chocolate in a microwave-safe bowl. Microwave on medium power for 1 minute then stir. Repeat the process, stirring after every 30 seconds until the chocolate has melted.

To melt chocolate on top of the hob: place the chocolate in a heatproof bowl that fits snugly on top of a saucepan. Bring a small quantity of water to a simmer in the saucepan and place the bowl on top. Reduce the heat and stir the chocolate until smooth and melted. Carefully remove from the heat and set aside.

To melt chocolate in the oven: place the chocolate in a heatproof bowl in an oven preheated to the lowest temperature or Gas mark. Stir occasionally until the chocolate has melted. This usually takes about 5–10 minutes.

Candied peel

Yield 200g (7oz)

4–6 **citrus fruits** (a mixture of grapefruit, oranges, lemons, limes), unwaxed and
    preferably organic (if not, wash fruit very well)
200g (7oz) **sugar**
200ml (7fl oz) **water**
100g (3½oz) **caster sugar,** for coating

Using a wide, horizontal vegetable peeler, peel the skin from the fruit, making sure not to peel away the bitter white pith. Finely slice the peel into matchsticks, or julienne strips. Set aside. Combine the sugar and water in a heavy-bottomed saucepan and bring to the boil. Boil the mixture gently until the sugar dissolves. Add the chopped peel, reduce the heat and simmer gently for 45 minutes. Remove the peel with a slotted spoon and place on kitchen paper to cool. Place the remaining sugar in a bowl. Toss the cooled peel in the sugar, then leave to dry on a clean tea towel.

Store in an airtight container. Candied peel will keep for several months.

Clear sugar glaze

A sugar glaze can give a cookie a shiny, glossy finish. Combine 1 part sugar to 2 parts water in a small saucepan. Bring to the boil then simmer over moderate heat for about 5 minutes or until reduced by half. Remove from the heat and allow to cool. To 3 Tbsp syrup add about 100g (3½oz) sifted icing sugar and mix until dissolved. Brush the glaze over still warm cookies and leave to set.

Stencil patterns

Stencil patterns can be bought from most kitchen shops or, alternatively, can be made easily at home. Use thin cardboard or baking parchment and cut out shapes or patterns. Hold the stencils over the cookies and gently sieve icing sugar or cocoa powder through a fine sieve to fill the uncovered surface. Gently remove the stencil and be careful not to stack the cookies. Make sure there is a contrast between the colour of the cookie and the dusting ingredient.

About the authors

New Zealand born Pippa Cuthbert's passion for food and cooking began at a very young age. With degrees in both Human Nutrition and Food Science, Pippa has gone on to build a successful career in London as a food stylist, food writer and home economist; working on books, magazines, TV commercials, packaging and advertorials. Complemented by each other's backgrounds, interests and skills, Pippa and Lindsay have now produced the sixth book in this series – Cookies!.

Food and writing are Lindsay Cameron Wilson's passions. She blended the two at university where she studied History, Journalism and the Culinary Arts. In 2001, Lindsay left her job as a food columnist in Halifax, Nova Scotia, and moved to London. That's when she met Pippa, and the work for their first book, *Juice!* began. Fueled by juice, the two moved on to *Ice Cream!*, *Soup!*, *Barbecue!*, *Pizza!* and now, their latest book in the series, *Cookies!*. Lindsay continues to work as a food journalist back in Canada, where she lives with her husband James, son Luke and baby Charlie.

Bibliography

Azevedo, Carla; *Una Casa Portuguesa, Portuguese Home Cooking* (Summerhill Press, 1990)

Cuthbert, Pippa and Cameron Wilson, Lindsay; *Ice Cream!* (New Holland, 2005)

Greenspan, Dorie; *Baking with Julia* (William Morrow, 1996)

Grimes, Lulu and Halsey, Kay; *Food – The Definitive Guide* (Murdoch Books, 2002)

Keller, Thomas; *Bouchon* (Artisan, 2004)

McGee, Harold; *On Food and Cooking* (Fireside, 1984)

Morton, Mark; *Cupboard Love – A Dictionary of Culinary Curiosities* (Bain & Cox, 1996)

Pastor, Carol; *Simple Home Baking* (New Holland, 2005)

Stewart, Martha; *The Martha Stewart Cookbook* (Random House, 1995)

Visser, Margaret; *The Rituals of Dinner* (Harper Collins, 1991)

Index